More Praise for *Deepening Community*

"Deepening community is essential to building healthy societies. Paul Born understands this principle and knows how to put it into practice. His book is an essential resource for everyone who wants to contribute to bringing forth better futures."
—**Adam Kahane, Partner, Reos Partners, and author of** *Solving Tough Problems*, *Power and Love*, **and** *Transformative Scenario Planning*

"There is no one writing today who understands more about community: what we miss when we don't have it, why we long for it, how to build it, and the rewards that it brings. Paul Born speaks to all of us in this book, at once touching our hearts and giving us the encouragement and the tools we need to change how we live in relation to those around us."
—**Dr. Frances Westley, cofounder of SiG (Social Innovation Generation), University of Waterloo, and coauthor of** *Getting to Maybe: How the World Is Changed*

"Community has the power to change everything. No amount of innovation, individual brilliance, or money can transform our broken society as effectively and sustainably as building community. *Deepening Community* provides useful and inspiring guidance for leaders everywhere who seek to create better outcomes in their work."
—**John Kania, Managing Director, FSG; founder of the Collective Impact Movement; and coauthor of** *Do More Than Give*

"Paul Born is a bright light. His commitment to community and celebration of life are infectious. If world leaders were to really embrace the principles of this book, we might be able to divert the social chaos and natural disasters of climate change. Put a copy of this book into the hands of an elected official or government leader near you!"
—**Nicole Rycroft, founder and Executive Director of the global environmental organization Canopy**

"Paul Born doesn't just study community; he lives it. In *Deepening Community*, he shares practical advice on how to reweave the social fabric that we have neglected for too long. This book exudes the joy he experiences in community, and his stories provide hope that, in this time of social, economic, and environmental crises, more of us will find ways to care deeply for one another and the place we share."
—**Jim Diers, faculty member, Asset-Based Community Development Institute, and author of** *Neighbor Power*

"Paul Born's call to deepen community in the face of fear and superficiality is steeped in the wisdom and insights of a remarkable life dedicated to helping people out of poverty. In a time of growing income disparity and social isolation, this timely book reminds us that there is a better way and that the joy to be found in taking it is there for everyone."
—**Stephen Huddart, President and CEO, J. W. McConnell Family Foundation**

"Paul Born has worked in community all his life with a watchful eye and an open heart, and he provides insights from what he has learned in *Deepening Community*—a must-read for anyone interested in strong communities."
—**Alan Broadbent, Chairman and CEO, Avana Capital Corporation; founder and Chairman, Maytree; and author of *Urban Nation***

"*Deepening Community* exudes joy. The joy of each other's company. The joy of belonging. The joy of taking care, of being cared for. Paul's book is also a joy to read. That is to be expected given Paul's life and work. He reminds us in print and in practice that joy is enduring, abundant, and beautiful."
—**Al Etmanski, social innovator, blogger, and author of *A Good Life***

"No one has helped me understand and value the essence of community like Paul Born. Paul has an amazing storytelling ability that excites, challenges, and demystifies and helps us all appreciate the simplicity of moving community from ideal to living reality. This book is a community builder's gem."
—**Peter Kenyon, Director, Bank of I.D.E.A.S. (Australia)**

"We need deep community to tackle issues such as environmental resiliency, a fair economy, and a safe and caring society. Paul confirms that we need enduring and trustful relationships for an even more fundamental reason: to be fully human. *Deepening Community* is an engaging and practical contribution to what may be the most important work of our times."
—**Mark Cabaj, social innovator and cofounder of Vibrant Communities Canada**

"This book is a testament to Paul Born's love of the hard work of building relationships and the joy it brings to us."
—**Ratna Omidvar, Preisdent Maytree, and named most influential leader of the decade by the *Globe and Mail***

Deepening Community

Deepening Community

FINDING JOY TOGETHER IN CHAOTIC TIMES

Paul Born

FOREWORD BY Peter Block

BK

Berrett–Koehler Publishers, Inc.
San Francisco
a BK Life book

Berrett-Koehler Publishers, Inc.
235 Montgomery Street, Suite 650
San Francisco, CA 94104-2916
Tel: (415) 288-0260 Fax: (415) 362-2512 www.bkconnection.com

Ordering Information
Quantity sales. Special discounts are available on quantity purchases by corporations, associations, and others. For details, contact the "Special Sales Department" at the Berrett-Koehler address above.
Individual sales. Berrett-Koehler publications are available through most bookstores. They can also be ordered directly from Berrett-Koehler: Tel: (800) 929-2929; Fax: (802) 864-7626; www.bkconnection.com
Orders for college textbook/course adoption use. Please contact Berrett-Koehler: Tel: (800) 929-2929; Fax: (802) 864-7626.
Orders by U.S. trade bookstores and wholesalers. Please contact Ingram Publisher Services, Tel: (800) 509-4887; Fax: (800) 838-1149; E-mail: customer.service@ingram publisherservices.com; or visit www.ingrampublisherservices.com/Ordering for details about electronic ordering.

Berrett-Koehler and the BK logo are registered trademarks of Berrett-Koehler Publishers, Inc.

Printed in the United States of America

Berrett-Koehler books are printed on long-lasting acid-free paper. When it is available, we choose paper that has been manufactured by environmentally responsible processes. These may include using trees grown in sustainable forests, incorporating recycled paper, minimizing chlorine in bleaching, or recycling the energy produced at the paper mill.

Library of Congress Cataloging-in-Publication Data
Born, Paul.
Deepening community : finding joy together in chaotic times / Paul Born; foreword by Peter Block. — First Edition.
    pages cm
Includes index.
ISBN 978-1-62656-097-0 (pbk.)
1. Community life. 2. Interpersonal relations. I. Title.
HM761.B67 2014
307—dc23   2013045214

First Edition

18 17 16 15 14   10 9 8 7 6 5 4 3 2 1

Cover design: M80 Design LLC / Wes Youssi
Interior design and composition: Leigh McLellan Design
Copyeditor: Elissa Rabellino

*To Jake Tilitzky, for building a community
that turned the pain of chaotic times into joy*

AND

*To Mom, Dad, my family,
and all the people at Eben Ezer,
for showing me that if we stay together,
look after each other, and work together
for a better world, we can thrive.*

Contents

Foreword

*t*HE IDEA OF COMMUNITY is all around us and increasingly on our lips. It sells real estate, markets social technology, and appears in the mission statements of most institutions. There are community recreation centers, community health movements, communities of practice, and community organizers. Unfortunately, the idea of community is more on our lips than in our experience. The speaking about community is always genuine, but it so goes against the individualism and fear embedded in our modern culture that it represents longing more than reality. It is more an adjective than a statement of central purpose.

The idea of community also suffers from its ambiguity. The word has a wide range of meanings. It can be a town, a network of interests, a neighborhood, a group of friends, or a set of employees. When a word covers everything, it loses its utility.

Paul Born, as much as anyone I know, has brought clarity and solid practical usefulness to this thing called community. He decided thirty years ago that if we care about poverty, safety, or well-being, then the experience of community is essential. It is the point. Not a luxury, or a pleasantry, or a memory of a time past. His work holds the intention that community needs to be at the center of our thinking, no matter what results we are trying to achieve in the world.

That is why this book, *Deepening Community*, is important. It should be required reading for all those, as Paul puts it, "who want to better understand the value of community and neighbors, and their importance in building belonging and inclusion into the services they offer or the social-change strategies they effect." In a personal and accessible way that is in total harmony with the book's message, Paul explains how to make community the heart of these efforts.

Making community the point is a major undertaking. It means we need to make the common good a priority again. It calls for cooperation and collaboration. It asks that we place the well-being of all of us higher than the well-being of any single one of us. If we take community seriously, then we agree to give up some control and to listen more than speak. Community blurs the line of where your property ends and mine begins. These are radical practices when taken seriously.

Western culture stands on a long history of affirming the rights of the individual. Capitalism worships the idea of competition and winning, so much so that we have raised the status of competition to be a defining part of our nature. We place a bell curve ranking the best to the worst over the heads of our children the moment they enter school.

In addition to revering competition and individualism, we hold a nearly religious belief in the healing effects of technology. As Paul declares, we believe the myth that "all we need is more time, money, and technology to solve the problems of peace, poverty, and health." Perhaps now is the time to put this myth to rest. This book invites us to do just that. It is an important invitation, and here is why:

- Time in the modern world has become the enemy of relatedness. Speed has become a rationalization for doing what we do not believe in. Time has become an argument against collaboration. Cooperation and democracy are discounted as inefficient. We live on the pretense of being busy.

- Money is also an argument against community. Learning together in the same room is costly. Meeting together is costly. The virtual world is justified by its low cost. We say, let's create the future online. We can learn online. We can meet online. This ignores the social and relational dimension of learning, the relational dimension of achievement. Learning and achievement have been reduced to a transfer of knowledge and automated ways of managing the world. When our occasions for human connection become commodified into what is cost-effective, so much for community. So much for relationships.

- Technology has become a religion, Steve Jobs a saint, and speed, convenience, global access, and home shopping a liturgy. The dominant argument against community, against the intimacy and connectedness that Paul speaks to, is that what was local, and intimate, and had space for silence, has now been automated. We have swallowed 24/7 as a condition of nature. We must respond, *this moment.* Wherever we meet, we bring our phones that we have labeled "smart." The technology manages us because it is there. In larger questions of the land, of the environment, of the workplace, technology promises nirvana. It replaces the schoolhouse and the local business. It promises connection, but in reality reinforces our isolation. We spend a lot of time alone, watching a screen.

Against this onslaught, *Deepening Community* radically declares that we *do* have the time, the money, and all the tools necessary to solve any challenge, by coming together in community. The book gives us the definitions we need. It makes important distinctions so that each of us can find our way into community, be it through inner work, family, neighborhood, or the workplace.

The book is also timely, for much is already occurring in the world that proves the value of community. There is a cohousing movement, where people choose to share the tasks of raising children, cooking, caring for the vulnerable, and keeping safe. There are pocket neighborhoods, such as those being designed by architect Ross Chapin: modest dwellings that all face a commons and become the village that raises a child.

There is a resurgence in cooperative businesses, where the well-being of the employees is their first priority and profit takes its rightful place as a means instead of an end. Every city has community gardens and community-supported agriculture networks (CSAs), where food is locally grown and abandoned land is reclaimed.

There is cooperative learning and cooperative education. A heart surgeon named Paul Uhlig has invented Collaborative Rounds, where the physician, nurses, and other supporting functions meet in a circle with the patient and family to jointly discuss treatment. When they do this, all measures of care improve. Edgar Cahn has developed TimeBanking, where generosity and neighborliness are tracked and exchanged. *Yes!* magazine does a beautiful job of telling the story of these movements toward community.

All these cooperative and communal ventures form a social movement of enormous importance, one that offers an alternative to the dominant belief in competition, materialism, and individualism. *Deepening Community* is an important contribution to this movement. The book is an anthem bearing witness to our humanity and our capacity to be together in peace. It takes a big step in making community building a legitimate discipline that belongs at the center of our thinking.

Peter Block
Cincinnati, Ohio

Preface

I N THIS BOOK I invite you to invest yourself in deepening community—to discover or rediscover the joy of being together.

I don't use the word *invest* lightly. Like any investment, community takes time and effort. We spend years investing for our retirement, setting aside dollars in order to live a good life in our old age. Our financial advisors tell us to start this process early, when we are young, in order to have enough when we're old (though they're always quick to add that it's never too late to start). Investing in relationships to deepen community reaps a similar benefit. A strong family, a faith community or club, neighbors we can rely on, and friends who make the hours pass quickly—these are equally worthy investments. The skills we learn by seeking and living in community, and the network of relationships we build, will provide us with the joy and security we need, especially should we experience times of loneliness, financial insecurity, or failing health.

I don't use the word *deepening* lightly, either. As I will explore with you in the pages that follow, I believe that we can deepen our experience of community as the alternative to falling into, or even embracing, dysfunctional forms of community: shallow community, based on selfish or even just lazy or bewildered individualism; and fear-based community, in which people derive their sense of belonging from anxiety or hatred.

I recognize that my call to deepen community makes my book a serious and even challenging one, but I believe that it also makes it a deeply joyful one. Why? Because of what I've seen in my work as a community activist, writer, and teacher: many of us, in response to environmental and economic worries, are going local and are rediscovering ourselves and one another. And rather than acting out of fear, we are finding purpose, belonging, security, and fulfillment, through the following:

- Enjoying one another

- Taking care of one another

- Working together to make our families, neighborhoods, communities, and the world great places to live in for all

We live in community. It's in our DNA. We need one another, plain and simple. Community shapes our identity and quenches our thirst for belonging. It helps us put life into perspective and sort out real danger from perceived danger. Community has the capacity to improve our physical, mental, and economic health, as well as our overall sense of happiness and fulfillment. It has the power to unite us all in a common bond as we work together for a better world.

I have written *Deepening Community* to empower all of us to open up to community, to make conscious choices about the kind of community we desire, and to feel more connected to the people we care about. Accordingly, I hope that this book will prove to be informative and stimulating to several types of readers:

- Individuals who want to deepen community in their lives and to contribute their talents and energy toward a common goal

- Parents who want to create a strong, life-sustaining community environment for their children

- Community-development professionals, faith leaders, and all those who want to better understand the value of community and neighbors, and their importance in building belonging and inclusion into the services they offer or the social-change strategies they effect

- Organizations and policy makers in search of a framework to enhance a sense of community and place for people

- Elected officials and bureaucrats who need to take notice and learn about citizen engagement and trust building as they keep the promises they've made

Throughout the pages that follow, I weave together three types of community stories. The first type comprises stories of the community I grew up in and the lessons it taught me. My people—a Mennonite community previously living in Ukraine—had suffered through one of the worst periods of history, when the entire world was at war. They survived because they stayed together. Although fear influenced their community, they thrived because they replaced their fear with love. The second concerns my experiences in the community-building work to which I've dedicated my life: thirty years, so far, of joining with others to bring people together to end poverty, work collaboratively, and harness the power of community. And the third type involves stories of many fellow seekers of deeper community whom I've met along the way.

The wonderful news is that the opportunity to deepen community is right in front of us—and so are the people who want to work with us to make it happen.

I Our Need Today for Deeper Community

In every community, there is work to be done.
In every nation, there are wounds to heal.
In every heart, there is the power to do it.

—MARIANNE WILLIAMSON, FOUNDER OF
THE PEACE ALLIANCE AND AUTHOR

MANY TIMES OVER the past thirty years, especially in connection with the work I've done with others more recently to engage communities in reducing poverty, I've been asked, "What is the most important thing people can do to make a difference in the world?"

"That's simple," I almost always reply. "Bring chicken soup to your neighbor."

"Really?" is the typical response.

I say yes, and then add, "But remember, I said the answer is simple. But the act of bringing soup . . . well, that takes work."

How so?

It requires that you know your neighbor.

It requires that you know they are not vegetarian and like soup.

It requires that you know them well enough and communicate regularly enough to know they are sick.

Once you know they are sick, you must feel compelled to want to help and to make this a priority among the many calls on your time and energy.

Your neighbor must know you well enough to feel comfortable in receiving your help.

And you must have enough of a relationship to know what they prefer when they are sick, whether it is chicken soup, *pho*, *chana masala*, or even ice cream.

So, you see, the work takes place long before you perform the act of bringing soup.

I think you would agree that the challenge, for so many of us today, is to find the time and energy and desire to do the work of being a good neighbor—even to stay close to members of our own family, for that matter. Many of us find ourselves stretched to keep in touch with one another, to share in one another's lives, to strengthen community together. I believe that a combination of the state of the environment and the economy, the stress of our jobs (or of finding a job), and the sped-up nature of life through new technologies is making it difficult for us to invest ourselves in community.

Do you ever feel this way?

Many people I know—including the five hundred people I surveyed in depth as I wrote this book (see the appendix) and the many I reach out to through my work and travels—have told me they want community to be less sporadic and more constant. They recognize that we are in danger of losing a sense of community in our lives. Even though we connect with people often, life today seems more complex than ever. Connecting, therefore, is sporadic and takes a lot of effort. For so many of us, our brothers and sisters and most of our cousins live a long way away, and even those who live nearby are so busy that we manage to connect with them only every month or two. With the exception of a few, the same goes for friends. To visit them means traveling long distances, which often is impractical.

Connecting with people sporadically doesn't feel right to us. More fulfilling would be the ability to show our caring when a friend is sick by going to their place and comforting them, knowing they would do the same for us. Somewhere within us we are aware that we need to deepen our experience of community. We know we should be sharing with family members, friends, and neighbors not just episodes of our lives but whole chapters and books and even libraries: we want to be part of the ongoing story of their lives, and we want them to be part of ours.

Now, it's not as if we never do these things. However, so many people have told me they would like community life to take less effort; they would like it to be a regular part of their daily life; they would like the connections they make to be natural extensions of their comings and goings, not relegated to deliberate actions that require extraordinary effort.

You would think that our neighborhoods would be natural places for building a deeper sense of community. This would be in stark contrast to the experience of being a neighbor today. Unless we are deliberate about meeting, we "hide" behind our apartment door dozens of floors up from a busy cityscape or behind a garage door that closes with a click of a button as we retreat to our suburuban oasis from the stresses of life. Many neighbors are so busy that they seldom even see one another coming and going. On weekends they're lucky to lay eyes on one another, as so many exit their weekday existence by cocooning or taking a quick trip away or heading for the cottage. Besides, we watch far too much TV and are involved in too many activities for our paths to cross.

Does any of the above describe your experience, at least to some degree? Are you like so many people I hear from who say they attend a community fundraiser or a neighborhood party and feel a sense of connection that evaporates as quickly as the event ends? They get involved by joining a church or a yoga class, but unless they attend weekly, they experience little connection outside the deliberate act of attending. Even when they join a committee or a midweek support group, the sense of community is confined to the place and time scheduled for the gathering. They may have a wonderful visit with a group of friends whom they have known for more than a decade but leave knowing it will be months (or years) before they do this again.

I do not want to express dissatisfaction with any of these moments in life. But that is exactly what they are: moments. We need not commit to anything more than the moment, and neither does anyone else. We have community, and then . . . well, it is gone, and we go on to the next experience of community. It is as though we have built deliberate barriers of time and place into our community interactions so that we can control how much community we experience and when we experience it. On the surface, this may sound ideal, but as much as we may enjoy this anonymity once in a while, it does not feel very satisfying in the long run.

The Possibilities of Community

I hope that you will join me in exploring the possibility of deeper community today. This book is my call to you—to us—to work together to deepen community: to make a conscious, proactive, intentional effort to hold on to and build on the connections between us, connections that will help us resist the pull of the often-neurotic social responses to the complexity of our times, what I will speak of in the next chapter as shallow community and fear-based community.

Community is not automatic, and it is not automatically optimal. We cannot take it for granted; we cannot assume that it is what it should be; we cannot stand on the sidelines and just hope that things will work out.

When we invest ourselves to deepen our experience of community, we can realize real benefits. Community can help shape our identity as a collective and interdependent people. It creates the opportunity for us to care for and about others and, in turn, to be cared for, the key interaction that builds a sense of belonging. When we belong and enjoy strong relationships with one another, we can rely on one another in both good and difficult times. This makes us more resilient, and it makes us healthier. It improves our economic opportunities (think about networking to find a job) and, as studies show, even makes us happier.

The Possibilities of Community for Our Children

My wife, Marlene, and I often wonder about the possibilities of community for our sons and what their memories of community will be when they are older. How will they know who they are and where they belong?

We spoke about this shortly after the birth of our first son, Lucas. For us, community was a defining understanding of how we wanted to raise our children; it was even reflected in the wording of our marriage vows. We committed ourselves to providing our children (Michael would follow, five years later) with as many "deep" experiences of community as we could. We went to church because it was a community. We attended reunions of our extended families, organized neighborhood barbecues, and helped out at a variety of schools and with a myriad of sports teams, because each of these represented community in our sons' lives.

We also spoke to them about community and its importance. For example, we shared a particular bedtime story with them many a night. I saw it as a nighttime prayer. As told to our son Michael, it went like this:

> Once upon a time there was a little boy, and his name was Michael, and everybody loved him: his mom, and his dad, and his brother [Michael interrupted me one night, piping up with, "That's not true, Dad; Lucas just likes me—he told me so"], his *oma* and *opa* [German for "grandma" and "grandpa"] and his *lola* [Filipino for "grandmother," which we called Marlene's mother after her sisters' families returned from four years of volunteer mission work in the Philippines], and all his cousins [a satisfied grin always covered Michael's face at this point; he really loved his cousins], and all the children at school, and everyone at his church [Michael always interjected "Not everybody," to which I would say, "Just about everybody," and he would say, "Yaaaa"], and all his neighbors [at which point Michael would beam and say, "Especially Dave and Marilyn; they have a pool"].

> And I would smile and give him a big hug and say, "Love ya," and Michael would say back, "Love ya, too. Goodnight."

Bridging the Self-to-Community Gap

Marlene and I want our children to have not only a positive self-identity but also a positive community identity. However, the complexity of our times makes living in community perhaps the biggest challenge we face.

I believe that Charles Dickens would not find it difficult to extend his description of the eighteenth century, in his novel *A Tale of Two Cities*, to our century, for we, too, live in the best of times and the worst of times.

For an example of the best of our times, consider how so many countries have come to understand the importance of the rights of every individual. We have embraced feminism and dismantled racism—or at least have built a broad social consensus against racist language and attitudes. We have welcomed gays and lesbians into greater participation in social institutions. We have spoken out against torture in war and violence toward children. There is a growing understanding today, from our youth on up, that we must care for those in need and fight the downward pull of hatred based on ethnicity and ideology. There is a growing consensus that we must work for a just society and the protection of the rights of the individual.

Is it possible, though, that the pendulum has swung too far? In making it a priority to enhance individual rights and opportunities, have we made it easier for people to ignore community responsibilities? Tracking along with the positive gains we have made with regard to individualism are examples of the worst of our times: when families struggle to find appropriate day care or schools, as if children were an individual responsibility, or when we walk past or even over the homeless, believing that they must have done something to deserve their plight. If someone were to win a million dollars, the world might say, "Good for you. Go ahead and spend it; you deserve it—it's yours." But our culture's individualistic approach does not bring deep satisfaction. Compare this with cultures in which people share windfalls with one another through potlatches or at large community weddings. Do we live in a time when an excessive focus on self is dismantling our need or sense of responsibility for one another?

We are tempted, when so much that comes at us is a mixture of the good and the bad, to throw up our hands in bewilderment and do nothing. But many individuals and groups are fighting against the worst-of-times aspects of life today. I see people of every socioeconomic bracket and faith and employment level struggling to make sense of the changes they're facing, desperately seeking a future for their children that is better than the one they see coming. They—we—are seeking new answers and, in turn, are finding deeper connections. For example, in an age of globalization, many of us are "going local." We're rediscovering local foods and gardening, the simple pleasures of walking and cycling, and our neighbors. Each connection we make in these contexts deepens our resolve. We're using the Internet to offer people who want to visit our cities a free or inexpensive week's stay in our homes. We're sharing services. Consider the "casual carpools" in the San Francisco Bay Area, whereby pedestrians line up in certain locations and, on the basis of trust, take the next car in line, driven by a stranger—no, by a fellow citizen.

Community has the power to change everything. We all know this. Whether in places where we work together; neighborhoods where we share emotional, physical, and cultural resources; or countries where we strive to live at peace, we must mobilize people to work together toward a common vision if we are going to deepen community for all.

The challenge, however, is not so much to find ways as groups to reach out to others as it is to bridge the gap from the self to the group in the first place. The challenge is to understand, and get past, our own sense of isolation. We embrace our culture's veneration of rugged individualism, acting in ways that Eastern cultures would see as selfish. How do we begin to turn this around? How do we make the connection from the self to others? How do we build a bridge between ourselves and others? How do we cross it?

My Experience of Community

I have learned a lot about community in my work at the Tamarack Institute, where we have helped many rediscover the power of community. This has resulted in a reduction of poverty for nearly 250,000 people. We are confident, as people in cities are reaching out, seeking deeper connection, and relearning the skills of community engagement and collaboration, that we will reach our goal of reducing poverty for one million families.

We have seen that people can learn and make choices to work together and to care together. That no matter how difficult the task, through community engagement and collaboration we can create a positive vision, organize ourselves to achieve it, and realize a better future for all. Our key learning? That even though it takes a lot of commitment and skill to change our cities, no amount of talent or hard work matters if people do not share a sense of community. The deeper the community, the easier and better the outcome.

I also learned a lot as I grew up in a small, mostly Mennonite farming community. We were not a cloistered group like the Old Order Mennonites or Amish but were similar in many of our beliefs. We (our parents) were refugees from Ukraine in the Soviet

Union who had come to Canada after World War II. Because of the deprivation and violence that we had experienced, we kept close to one another. Eben Ezer Mennonite, our church of about four hundred people, was both the social and spiritual center of our lives. We were a community that was trying to heal and establish itself in a newfound country. I grew up feeling a tremendous sense of warmth, identity, and belonging, which was the foundation of my later understanding of community.

In my late teens, I studied to be a minister. Even though I quickly realized that this was not for me (I often joke that I like sin too much), I learned a lot during that time about the ideal of living a simple life with others. This experience gave me an intellectual understanding of community and inspired me to seek out and hear the stories of communities from many traditions.

In the 1980s, not long after we married, Marlene and I moved into our first home, on a small street in Cambridge, Ontario, in Canada. There our sons grew up with loving neighbors. Many of the families on that street celebrated holidays and birthdays together, swam together in the one pool on the street, and supported one another in the rearing of children. This profoundly shaped my understanding and adult experience of community.

Family has always been central to community for me and a source of many insights. The family I grew up in, and my extended family of cousins and uncles and aunts, influenced me profoundly. Marlene and our sons are amazing, fun, and supportive. And now Marlene's cousins and aunts and uncles—who publish a regular family newsletter called The Eppisode (the title refers to their last name, Epp)—are teaching me about community and bringing it into my life.

I have been blessed with jobs in great workplaces, with colleagues who collaborate to build neighborhoods and improve communities to make the world a better place. Deep friendships have formed among us as we have worked together, committing ourselves to one another and a cause. While helping others to build community, we ourselves have become a community through our jobs, potlucks, celebrations, and parties.

The church I have attended for the past decade is filled with warm and caring people. Most have attended the church since they were children and have a deep sense of place there. The building is beautiful and the music heavenly. My primary reason for belonging, however, has not been to attend Sunday-morning worship services; it has been to gather with the community, to pray and reflect and be hopeful with others, to share in their lives and they in mine.

I feel community with friends who live in my city and with many who no longer do. Other communities in my life include the social circles Marlene and I belong to and my yoga studio.

Seeking Community

However, like so many people I hear from these days, I can feel isolated in the midst of a crowd. Even though I am surrounded by people I care about, I can feel alone, with less community in my life than I want. I realize that loneliness, fear, and a desire for happiness are constants in the human condition. Each one contributes to the feeling of being alone, though it is not always easy to see a direct cause-and-effect relationship.

Why do I—why do we—seek community when there are so many people in our lives?

A helpful analysis of the situation I find myself in—of the situation many of us find ourselves in—comes from the social critic Christopher Lasch, who wrote *The Minimal Self: Psychic*

Survival in Troubled Times to explore what he saw as a society-wide response to perceived threat. He describes life for those facing the threat of cosmic disaster, which, in the context of his times (he wrote the book in the mid-1980s), meant the nuclear arms race, terrorism, and rising crime:

> People take one day at a time. They seldom look back, lest they succumb to a debilitating "nostalgia"; and if they look ahead, it is to see how they can insure themselves against the disasters almost everybody now expects. Under these conditions, selfhood becomes a kind of luxury, out of place in an age of impending austerity. Selfhood implies a personal history, friends, family, a sense of place. Under siege, the self contracts to a defensive core, armed against adversity. Emotional equilibrium demands a minimal self, not the imperial self of yesteryear.

Our times are not that different from Lasch's, though we could add to his list of threats a marked increase in terrorism; the Internet's intensification of consumerism and challenge to our sense of self, through the conflation of public and private; and climate change. I believe that his analysis casts light on why we find community difficult today. It is far easier for us to flit from site to site on the Internet, to define ourselves by who and what we "like," to create a sense of self by what we buy and wear and use, than it is to build and sustain connections with one another in space and time. In some ways it is ironic that we call this activity "social" media when so much of it is created by individuals sitting alone at their computers or with their smartphones.

That said, many young people are building connections through the Internet, cleverly and determinedly finding ways to connect cybernetic and bricks-and-mortar community. (For example, see Lucas's story in chapter 5.) As I know from my own work as a community activist, social media can be used to bring people together to celebrate or work on a common cause. However, this capability is ever in danger of succumbing to another element in our lives: our emphasis on individualism at the cost of community.

Defining, Choosing, and Making Community

I believe that today the onus is on us to define community, to choose community, to make community. Yes, this is a far piece from the simplicity of earlier times in which people's experience of community was defined by the circumstances of their birth—their family and place of birth. I accept that, today, community is largely situational. It changes at different stages of our lives. I might be very active in a spiritual community and have a tremendous sense of belonging, but then, after some time, that changes. I might play basketball with a group of guys every Thursday evening but have to accept that this is as far as I'm going to get in those men's lives. As a way of dealing with the fragmented feel of modern life, I am learning to take comfort in knowing that I do not need to hold on to one community, or even to consider one community my primary community—that there are many experiences of community.

I persist, however, in believing that deeper community is possible and may be engaged in at the same time. That finding joy together even in chaotic times is a real possibility. I am privileged, in my work, to witness people coming together to reduce poverty and to make their neighborhoods safe. I have seen ecosystems restored. I have seen food systems made more secure. And I have seen fear overcome. That is why I have written this book: to encourage us to do the work of community, to perform the "supply chain" of efforts and acts that lead to the point at which we hand that bowl of chicken soup to an indisposed neighbor.

Specifically, in the next chapter, I explore the three community options—shallow community, fear-based community, and deep community. I follow that discussion with chapters on how we can turn away from fear, how we can turn toward deeper community, and how we can embrace the four acts of community life:

- Sharing our stories
- Taking the time to enjoy one another
- Taking care of one another
- Working together for a better world

2 Three Options for Community in Challenging Times

We are our choices.

—JEAN-PAUL SARTRE, TWENTIETH-CENTURY
FRENCH PHILOSOPHER

*W*E MIGHT DRAW an analogy to the possibilities of community in times like ours from psychoanalyst Karen Horney's description, in the early part of the twentieth century, of the coping mechanisms of individuals. In her book *Our Inner Conflicts: A Constructive Theory of Neurosis,* Horney argues that individuals relate through one of three main interpersonal strategies; these three may be summarized as follows:

DETACHMENT:

- *Moving away from others*—seeking personal autonomy or narrowing one's personal boundaries to avoid others

AGGRESSION:

- *Moving against others*—seeking power over others, exploiting others, or vying for personal achievement or social recognition at the cost of others

COMPLIANCE:

- *Moving toward others*—seeking the affection or approval of others and working together to solve problems

Similarly, we relate to community in one of three main ways:

- *Turning away from others* and accepting or even embracing shallow community
- *Turning against others* through the building of fear-based community
- *Turning toward others* and working together to create deep community

Which option will we choose: shallow community, fear-based community, or deep community?

The following table shows the characteristics of the three community options, which will be explored throughout this book. The dysfunctional approaches to community are shown in columns one and two, and the approach to deep community is shown in column three.

It seems to me that deciding not to make the effort to build community together and setting up false community based on an ideology are both responses to massive change in societies the world over. That is, we respond to the confusing and overwhelming phenomena coming at us in an increasingly complex world through shallow community or fear-based community.

Allow me to paint a picture of society today to help us understand these two responses.

Contemporary technologies, primarily digitalization and the Internet, have shrunk our world, making all events and all problems omnipresent to us. Nations and individuals reach out for our overstretched attention as we sit in front of our TV or computer. In effect, we are all media editors of a sort: we choose from the plethora of images and sound bites on our televisions, computers, and phones and sequence them to make up the film and soundtrack of our lives.

SHALLOW COMMUNITY	FEAR-BASED COMMUNITY	DEEP COMMUNITY
This is my story. Entertained, no emotional bond.	I am not one of them.	To open doors between us. Stories unite us.
Hedonism. Friends we see once a month, family at Christmas. We have association but lack bonding.	Join others against others. We are right and they are wrong. We must stop them.	Knowing one another by spending repeated time together. Celebrate together in person, children know and trust us.
Take care of yourself— no one else will. Send a get-well card, phone on their birthday, post a birthday message on Facebook. Our doctor cares for us when we are sick.	Believe that "we" have a greater right to life (happiness) than "they" do. We are stronger when they are weaker.	Mutual acts of caring build a sense of belonging. We know and act when neighbors and friends and family are sick. Mutual acts of caring occur often.
I am alone in this world. Send in a donation, click "Like" on Facebook, sponsor a child in Africa, yet do not know names of children next door.	Share a belief that we are right and they are wrong, and work together to realize that belief. If we work together, we can win and they will lose. I will do whatever it takes for my "tribe," or people, to win and defeat the other.	Share a belief that creates a benefit for all, act together for the benefit of all. An absence of "they" or "them." As we care for others, our caring for each other deepens.

Besides this effect of personal and global communication, we are increasingly part of a global economic ecosystem. A well-known illustration of chaos theory about the natural order holds that a butterfly flapping its wings in one part of the world causes a hurricane to form elsewhere, days later. I see this as an analogy to the state of the world economy today. The failure of a banking system in one part of the world tanks markets in Europe just days later. And as for the natural order itself, the ecosystem is straining under humanity's overproduction and catastrophic mistakes: for example, more than a thousand sick sea lion pups came in with the tide on the shores of Southern California in 2013; scientists are researching the possible link between this phenomenon and the nuclear plant meltdown in Fukushima, Japan, two years earlier.

Further, in our unguarded moments we sometimes wonder what would happen if the world's economic and natural ecosystems failed at the same time. We avert our eyes from dire reports, such as one from senior policy advisor José Riera of the United Nations predicting that by 2050, between 250 million and one billion citizens could be displaced from or within their countries as a result of drought and war.

The fear that the world will end in our lifetime causes us to throw away our lightbulbs and buy more sustainable replacements that were shipped in from who knows where. More personally, when we read the newspaper, we get a sense that there is one more thing we need to do or we will die. Though we respect the experts and want to live a healthy and responsible life, it is becoming a bit much. Medical fears top the list for many of us. Drink green tea and wine and eat dark chocolate and you will live a long life, we are told—and if you do not, you will get cancer and die!

Add terrorism alerts and emergency closings of embassies, and it's enough to make us consider building an environmentally approved bomb shelter, filling it with locally grown organic food, and hunkering down until it's over.

OPTION ONE   *Shallow Community*

So how do we respond to all this? One way is to be satisfied with shallow community. Years of embracing individualism and consumerism and relying on outside or professional intervention to meet our needs have left many of us with few resources for deepening community. For sure, we are rusty. We go from one group activity to the other seeking connection and personal fulfillment and are so often left wanting more and seeking the next "great experience." These experiences are shallow not because they are fun or entertaining but because they do not require ongoing connection and mutual caring.

I often think of those famous words written by John Donne more than four centuries ago: "No man is an island, entire of itself; every man is a piece of the continent, a part of the main." If Donne were writing today, would he tweet the words "Each man is an island, entire of himself"?

Many of us succumb to the temptation to be content with shallow community. We may do so as a defense mechanism: we may simply wish to get away from the bewildering waves of information crashing on our shores. Ironically, demands for community through the cacophony of voices presenting choices by which we may define the presence of community in our lives cause some of us to say enough and pull down the curtains. We build a community of the self to find peace from the complexity outside us. For example, we may devote ourselves to pleasure or autonomy or personal perfectionism as we style ourselves by what we "like" in social media, by what we buy on the Internet and in stores, by the houses we live in, by the cars we drive, by the trips we take.

Of course, any of these attempts can have dire consequences.

- A search for personal peace may be doomed in a world that is at once intimately connected and deeply fragmented.

- The pursuit of pleasure can create a vacuum that we fill by abusing pleasure, through alcohol, drugs, or sex.

- Perfectionism may seem an innocent desire, but its context—our imperfect world—can cause a dangerous gap to form between our desires and reality.

- And consumerism can waste natural resources, create inequity among those who produce what we consume, and distance us from the real nature of people, whom we begin to define on the basis of surface issues—their consumer choices.

Shallow community may be an attempt—conscious or not—to deny our innate desire for deeper community. Or it may be a decision—again, conscious or not—to avoid making the effort to deepen community. Finally, it may be the simple choice—conscious or not—to be content with living a life with little commitment. Individual experiences or choices may be valid in and of themselves, but they may, in the end, add up to living for oneself, in the moment, with little consideration for others.

OPTION TWO   *Fear-Based Community*

A community based on fear is a dangerous place.

These communities are real, and they are growing. They are built by people who are trying to make sense of changes outside their control and their comfort zone. In turn, they position themselves against the other to feel safe or hopeful. They do not accept people for who they are but require them to unite against someone or something as the price of belonging. Fear-based communities derive their sense of reality from being against community; they exist only on the basis of creating an enemy or developing a "them against us" narrative. Examples include the following:

- Damaging the property of a company because it is polluting the earth.

- Angrily opposing the actions of another religion, calling it immoral or a cult, which can feel righteous but cause children to hate other children at school. We fear another person's choice because we believe in the choices we have made. This fear can grow out of control quickly when groups start to organize against the other side. Fear becomes irrational, and in extreme cases violence follows.

- Setting up gated communities like the one where Trayvon Martin was shot. Twin Lakes residents said that there had been dozens of reports of attempted break-ins, which had created an atmosphere of fear in their neighborhood. Was the fear that caused George Zimmerman to shoot the same fear that caused him to live in a gated community in the first place?

- Turning a blind eye as poverty-stricken neighborhoods become places of fear after dark, when gangs and drugs and prostitution come to life. Crime is both a response to and a result of fear: a response because it is a short-term solution to poverty, a result because crime causes people to close their doors and ignore one another in the hope that their anonymity will keep them out of harm's way.

- Breeding fear through injustice. When injustice is perceived as systemic or against "my people," as we have seen in Palestine, Northern Ireland, and Somalia, it can turn citizens into terrorists, people who feel that revenge or acts of war will make them safer.

- Reacting to full-scale systemic changes in ways that make them even worse. Changes in the environment are an important example of fear-based belonging: As water shortages increase, rising sea levels and an increasing number of storm-induced disasters cause people to be afraid and vulnerable. As they search for safety together, more and more people migrate to safer climates, putting those places at ecological risk and sparking one of the oldest drivers of violence: the fear that someone is taking what is rightfully ours.

I used to think that these fears had always been with us, and I was always certain that we would get through them. I still believe that we will get through them, but I'm not convinced that the troubles are the same as before. Things are going to get worse before they get better. And no amount of innovation or brilliance will save us from the pain that the getting worse is going to cause.

Some may consider my outlook unwarranted, arguing that we can just forge ahead because, surely, innovations are near to hand and will help us address any challenge we might face.

It is true that new technologies have made it possible for us to live efficiently in large cities. They have enabled us to produce food and supply water to sustain ourselves. We are able to monitor almost every aspect of our humanity from our computers and smartphones. In a matter of hours, we can visit one another anywhere on the globe. Science, we are told, is en route to curing every major disease and solving every possible disaster. When this we-can-fix-it faith is challenged, the reply is confident: all we need is more time, money, and technology to overcome the problems of war, poverty, and health. We are asked to affirm ourselves as a people of possibility, a people without limits.

But for most of us, this faith is shaken by the realization that unfettered growth and overpopulation are unsustainable. The human spirit is increasingly uncertain and fearful. More and more of us have learned to question the amazing advancements of our times.

We know that the scientific and communications developments of the twentieth century and our nascent century have improved our health and made connecting with one another more efficient. Despite all that remains to be done, longer life expectancy *has* come to some countries that are working their way to better nutrition.

But we also know that the previous century was the bloodiest in history, one in which totalitarian nations on the left and the right slaughtered or starved their own people and those outside their borders—and did so on a scale and with a rigor precisely made possible by ever-more-sophisticated science and technology. Today, we see other nations picking up the worst practices of twentieth-century countries: today, different people cower in their homes, fearing the knock on the door, or the knocked-down door, that presages torture and death. New killing fields are being tilled. Weapons of mass destruction still go to the highest bidder—or sometimes are provided at no cost, framed as part of a geopolitical strategy.

Humanity seems to be divided between those who welcome change and those who abhor it. Yet, today, even those in the former camp, loath as they may be to see our times as chaotic, are aware that the changes we are undergoing could well end up being destructive. Most of us are aware that far too many societies and nations define community on the basis of fear. Think of the complexity of factions in various Middle Eastern countries, fueled by ideological enmity and paranoia to terrorize and kill one another and those beyond.

Fear can bind us together like nothing else. When we are afraid together, we make sense of what is going on around us by creating an us-versus-them reality in which the threat is quickly heightened. We build a community based on our fear and experience a sense of belonging in our mutual purpose. The greater our commitment against the other, the greater our solidarity.

OPTION THREE   *Deep Community*

Ironically, one of the main conflicts in our world today may be seen as a battle between the two options discussed above. Some countries, religions, and ideologies form community based on their fear and hatred of the shallowness of other countries, religions, and ideologies. Furthermore, both of these options may be defined as dysfunctional responses to a desire for deep community. That is to say, shallow community is a turning away from the challenge of building deep community, and fear-based community is a misguided attempt to build deep community.

What about this third option, then? What about what this book calls us to do: to consciously make the effort, individually and together, to deepen community?

To deepen community is to find opportunities for ongoing connection with those we care about and those who care about us. This connection strengthens the bonds between us. It builds an emotional resilience within and between us that, in turn, builds mutuality and reciprocity. We begin to open ourselves up to receive and give. Mutual acts of caring become the basis of an ever-stronger feeling of belonging.

This type of deep community can be found in the following places:

- In our neighborhoods, when we look out for one another's children or give our neighbors peace of mind by bringing in their mail while they're on vacation, along with watering their garden and watching for anything suspicious.

- In our extended families, where brothers and sisters and aunts and uncles vacation together every year—cooking together and telling stories of family and events through the decades—a tradition that leads them to interact all year long, celebrating birthdays, visiting and caring for one other when they are sick, and enjoying one another's company to avoid a lonely weekend.

- In our community associations or sports teams, as we gather weekly to support one another, play together, and build a stronger team—activities that lead us to care about, and reach out to, one another in times of need or to work together to raise funds for others in need so that they can enjoy these same activities with us.

- In our faith communities, where we share a belief and support one another through life struggles—sharing a potluck meal after the worship service, having gone to great lengths to prepare the best food possible as an act of love for the people who make the place where we meet not just a building but a community; helping to teach and rear one another's children; celebrating weddings together and mourning together at funerals, opening our hearts to one another, building a reciprocity and a sense of belonging.

- In a community organization where we volunteer or work and build deep community around a cause or hope. As we work together to build something better for those beyond us, as we open our hearts to those in need, we bond together, and the warmth of commitment, the altruism we express collectively, causes a form of connection that makes our commitment strong and the work light.

When we develop deep community, we can overcome our loneliness and challenge our fear; we can come together to make sense of the destruction around us; we can reach out together and actually do something about it.

I believe that there are four acts that individually and especially together deepen community: sharing our story, enjoying one another, taking care of one another, and working together for a better world. Later, beginning with chapter 5, I devote a chapter to each act, but let me touch on each one of them here.

ACT 1   Sharing Our Story

Deepening community starts when we share our story as a way of opening up to one another. Deep community comes from a commitment to be in relationship with others. To want to know and engage in the unfolding stories of people over time. To be a part of their lives as they suffer or have moments of joy. To want to be part of their story even if it is messy and inconvenient—or maybe because it is so. To want others to be part of our story in the same way; to laugh together, to cry, and to have disagreements

and to make up. To want this type of relationship with our families and neighbors and friends present and future.

ACT 2: Enjoying One Another by Spending Time Together

Deepening community means spending time together with others
over time, making these experiences as simple and easy as going
next door and visiting with a neighbor without having to be invited.
Being able to drive up to the cottage and visit family and know
they are always expecting us. Laughing together and knowing
how to have fun together, playing games or perpetrating practical
jokes. Deepening community is the desire to feel safe, knowing
that we are part of a community together, that we have our good
points and bad and yet are accepted for who we are—yes, at times
judged, and yes, at times gossiped about, but never ignored and
always included. Deepening community means knowing that,
with these people, we belong.

ACT 3 Caring for One Another

Deepening community also involves creating places and opportunities where we can care for others: community life in which
people expect something of us. If they are sick, they can expect
us to call, to drop in on them and bring them chicken soup or,
to soothe a bad back, a bottle of Scotch. In return, we can know
that when we get sick, we will be cared for and visited and made
to feel that others want us to get well so that we can spend time
together.

Deepening community means creating opportunities for these
experiences of caring and being cared for to be constant: to fight

over who pays the check, to be the first to call and say "I'm sorry," to not worry about who got invited last. It means knowing that we will be there for one another when they, and when we, are in need; that if our children marry, we will help one another celebrate; that when we retire, they will care for us and we for them; and that if we die before they do, they will be at our funeral. Deepening community is knowing that we belong.

ACT 4 Working Together to Build a Better World

And then, when we know and trust one another, we can work together to build the community we are part of. The deepest experience of community is the privilege to work together with others to make things better for someone else and for one another. To care about the same things with others and to wish for, and work for, the betterment of those in need. In this way, we become more than we can be by ourselves and together can be something we all are proud of.

To restore that which is broken is to truly challenge our fear. Option three, deepening community, is to reach out and build the relationships that will help realize our longing for belonging and true safety: not just relationships but networks of relationships that we invest in, surrounding ourselves with people we care about and who care for us. This investment pays great dividends: it helps us combat loneliness and fear, and it helps us see a clear difference between true community and false community.

I hope that community can be more than an ideal, that it can be a living reality that permeates our everyday lives. I hope that community will find us not just because we seek it but also because we are living in ways that make it unavoidable. I hope that community will be a priority and a valued way of living, as important to individuals, groups, and society as good health, financial security, and social status.

But hope is not a strategy in and of itself. It needs to be based on a mutual understanding of what we want, of what we hope, together.

We have a choice. We can make a difference. We can build deep community together.

3 Turning Away from Fear

Fear is the cheapest room in the house.
I would like to see you living in better conditions.

—KHWAJEH SHAMS AL-DIN MUHAMMAD
HAFEZ-E SHIRAZI, FOURTEENTH-CENTURY
MYSTIC AND POET

I WANT TO TELL YOU the story of a community, my community, because it was shaped by fear—and for good reason—but
found a way to use that fear to help others, experiencing great
joy in the process. I hope that this story will give us the strength
to challenge our fears in these times, as well as ideas for how to
overcome our fear of those we perceive to be the problem.

Living in Fear

I grew up afraid. Not every day. The truth was much deeper than
any particular experience or threat. Fear had embedded itself
deep in my soul. I breathed fear, and fear shaped who I became.
This type of irrational fear is shared by so many around the world
in a time characterized by displacement, whether voluntary or
involuntary. That is why it is so difficult to keep fear from defining
community.

"The communists are coming!" For my community, this was a statement based on experience, not a vague anxiety. This fear was seldom expressed verbally, but it deeply affected the way my family and community lived their daily lives.

My parents and the several hundred other Mennonites who emigrated to our community in Abbotsford, British Columbia, from Ukraine after World War II shared a Mennonite mantra. Not "I think, therefore I am," but "We flee; that's just the way it is."

Mennonites had been hunted and killed ever since the sixteenth century, when our founders, including Menno Simons, after whom we are named, refused to put any credence in their children's, and their own, baptism as infants by the Roman Catholic Church. Called Anabaptists—with ana meaning "again"—they believed that the Bible taught that only voluntary "true believers" should be baptized. Because children were too young to make such a decision, baptism was to be reserved for adults. The Anabaptists stirred up a big problem. At the time there was little daylight in most countries between baptism into the church and membership in the society or state. The Mennonites believed that there should be a very clear separation between church and state. It is a long and complicated story, but, in short, the Mennonite way of thinking led to a lethal conflict between them and the religious and political authorities.

In the late eighteenth century, at the invitation of Catherine the Great, Czarina of the Russian Empire, my ancestors settled in the fertile steppes of Ukraine. There they lived in relative peace, and eventually immense prosperity, for more than a hundred years. By the late nineteenth century, some Mennonites had moved to Canada and the United States. But not my family.

Then, early in the twentieth century, the communists arrived, bringing revolution and chaos. Roving bandits and the warring Red and White armies put the Mennonites in their crosshairs:

many were killed; at times whole villages were massacred. Though the Mennonites were pacifists by tradition, some were so frustrated and desperate that they fought back with small armies of their own.

After communism became the ruling system, the Mennonites, being land and factory owners, were forced to live on collective farms. Their churches and schools were closed, and their way of life was destroyed.

When Joseph Stalin took power in 1924, he was determined to force all of Ukraine to conform. In the reign of terror that ensued, the Mennonites were so beaten and afraid that some turned informant, betraying their neighbors to secure their own release from prison. Many Mennonites, including both of my grandfathers, were picked up at night and charged with treason—mainly for having Bibles in their possession—and were executed shortly after.

Stalin's most vicious attack was his failure to relieve the region during the famine of 1932–1933, in which millions of Ukrainians died: some say this was a deliberate genocide to tame the rebellious region. My parents, my older cousins, and all the adults in the church in which I was raised survived this massive trauma, only to see Ukraine destroyed by the German attack on the Soviet Union during World War II. Though others were deeply affected, calm and stability reigned for the Mennonites for a few years under German occupation. The Mennonites, most of whom still spoke German, hated the communist political system; they had suffered so much at the hands of the Soviets that they saw the Germans as saviors. Indeed, the Germans allowed them to return to private farming and to reopen their churches and schools. Later, when sharing their stories of this time, most Mennonites said that they had not been aware of the German death camps and the ensuing Holocaust. Probably some did know.

In 1944, the tables turned again, when the Soviets got the upper hand over the Germans. As the latter retreated, they invited the

Mennonites and other people of German background to go with them. The Mennonites, fearing the severe repercussions they would face at the hands of the Soviets for having collaborated with the enemy, fled the country. Many young men, including my father, were recruited at gunpoint at the end of the war to fight for the German army on the Russian front. As the Red Army caught up to the fleeing refugees, thousands were killed or sent back to gulags in the Soviet Union.

From 1948 to 1950, about eight thousand Mennonites emigrated to Canada—mostly women and children, because by this time the majority of the adult males had been killed or exiled. The book *Women Without Men: Mennonite Refugees of the Second World War*, written by Marlene Epp, traces this story.

Of the several hundred families that settled in Abbotsford, British Columbia, about a hundred of them, my parents included, eventually formed the Eben Ezer Mennonite Church. The name came from the Old Testament story of the ancient Jews who rested after their escape from Egypt and their wanderings in the desert at a place to which they gave this name, which means "God has led us thus far" (1 Samuel 7:12). Is it any wonder that I grew up feeling that Canada was a stopover, rather than my home; that we could and probably would be displaced, and sooner rather than later? Surely the communists (or someone else) would come, bringing destruction and death, and we would flee yet again—to another country, to a safer place. We saw ourselves, by definition, as displaced persons.

My parents and their friends had witnessed and experienced horrible things, and many had been forced to do horrible things. The need for support and healing bound our church congregation together. We prayed, sang, ate, worked, and played our way through the terrible memories, trying to make sense of our suffering.

Probably the most important thing we did was shape our identity. Together, we counteracted the negative effects of fear by building a healthy worldview that served us well. Our community's network of relationships and our practice of mutual caring helped us manage our fear and shape our common and individual identities. Without community, most of our parents would have ended up hardened and depressed, and most of us, their children, would have become angry and bitter.

At first we were a community of poor farmers struggling to feed our families. But that did not last long. Though we did not own things collectively, we supported one another, sharing ideas and opportunities. If one farmer learned something innovative about raising chickens, the next thing you knew, all of us had several thousand chickens and were sharing use of the same feed company and egg-grading station. We learned about land development, about building houses, about buying and selling secondary farms. We prospered—together.

Belonging

I was reminded of my own early experiences of my community's pilgrimage during a leadership course I took recently. We participants were given paper and different colors of markers to draw a lifeline. This was to help us understand our "mental models" and "ladders of influence"—how we think about the world and what experiences and influences have shaped our thinking. I was surprised by how vibrantly I drew my growing-up years. I used a lot of green, symbolizing growth and joy.

In the group discussion that followed, I shared that my childhood was filled with a sense of community. I was asked to recall the first time I experienced this feeling. It didn't take long for me to remember, and then retell with great enthusiasm, the story of an annual pig-butchering day held on my family's farm.

I was six years old, a big, strong boy with dark hair, chubby red cheeks, a huge smile, and an ample belly. I was excited by the prospect of a break from the daily routine of gathering the eggs, feeding the animals, and tending the garden.

Pig-butchering day started early. Extended-family members, neighbors, and friends (in our case, these were often the same people) congregated at our farm and started setting up. The tasks for the day included cutting the meat into roasts and chops, extracting hams and ribs, and packaging what was left to make pork sausage, liver sausage, ground pork, and headcheese (don't ask).

Heinz Giesbrecht was a central figure in the butchering. He was the most knowledgeable about the process and carried many of the recipes in his head. We all called him Uncle Heinz, even though he was my dad's uncle. The shortage of adult males in our community, as a result of the war and Stalin's purges in Ukraine, often simplified relationships. Because of his gentle nature, I always imagined Uncle Heinz, the senior male in our extended family, as my grandfather.

Lunch was special on pig-butchering day. A long table was set up for everyone present to enjoy a meal together. On this particular day, Uncle Heinz asked me to sit beside him while we ate. I enjoyed the special attention that he showed me.

On the table were loaves of my mother's famous fresh crusty white bread and Kotletten mit Eadschok mit Schmaunt Fat: meatballs made with ground beef and pork, mixed with garlic and onions and salt and pepper, fried in bacon fat, and smothered with a jar of rich, fresh cream mixed with what my mother called the "juice" left over from the frying—all of this served on top of potatoes. I would not recommend this meal for heart health, but let me tell you, on a cold fall day, after a morning of hard work, it was a real treat.

After a prayer, said at length by my dad, we all dug in and filled our plates with meatballs and potatoes, pouring generous helpings of creamy gravy over it all. As the meal was ending, Uncle Heinz saw that I had finished the potatoes and meatballs but still had plenty of gravy on my plate. He leaned over and said, "Paul, today I am going to teach you to be a man." Whereupon he passed me a piece of bread and showed me how to scoop up every last drop of the gravy and eat the bread. My plate was clean and dry.

That moment, more than any other, brings back deep memories of community. Yes, pig-butchering day was a communal effort to prepare food for the winter. Yes, it was a time to be with family, creating a sense of togetherness. Yes, it was a day of giving to the less fortunate at home and overseas through Mennonite Central Committee (MCC). And yes, it was an occasion for elders to teach the ways of a people to children. But for me, this day was special because of an uncle's gesture that told me who I was and where I belonged. Cleaning my plate spoke volumes about who we were as a community: simple and frugal farmers who had survived near-starvation in a frigid climate and near-death in a hostile political climate.

I knew who I was, and that I was needed, and that I needed everyone who was there. We had endured not because of our individual efforts but because we had stayed together. Children were reared, people were helped, and work got done—together. No matter how bad things got, as long as we had one another, we could survive and even thrive.

These experiences shaped my identity as a refugee, as an underdog who would need to work hard to succeed in life. Frugality and simple living, sharing and faith—these became a deep part of me.

A Caring-Based Community

Small wonder that I grew up identifying with the story of the Chosen People's exodus from Egypt and forty-year search for community. It was my story. While studying to become a pastor, I wrote a paper that focused on the approximately one dozen biblical passages that describe a particular command to the Jews: "You were once ger in the land of Egypt; therefore treat the ger in your land as you would have wanted to be treated." The Hebrew word ger is loosely translated as "strangers, sojourners, wanderers in the land."

This directive was part of what led me to a career in community development. I suppose that taking this career path may have been a way to ensure the security of my family, my people. If we do good to others, maybe, just maybe, God will keep the communists from invading Canada and we will all be safe.

The death and destruction experienced by the Mennonites is more than any one people should have to endure. Our fear provided the context for how we organized ourselves: the work we did, the food we ate, the friends we made, the things we did when we were not working.

We were farmers, and so were most of the Mennonites with whom we went to church. We were farmers not only because that was what most of us knew and had done in Ukraine but also because farming enabled us to be more independent: we could live off the crops we grew and the livestock we kept; the skills we had acquired would hold us in good stead should disruption come. Farming was a highly transferable skill for self-preservation.

Each summer my family filled our cellar with jar upon jar of canned fruits and vegetables. We canned watermelon, cucumbers, peaches, apricots, and cherries, and made relishes from carrots and cabbage. The summer cellar in our basement was huge and certainly the most important feature of our home. Along with our kitchen, it was our home's inner sanctum. Next to this cellar were two massive freezer chests, each the size of a small car, which we filled with the pig and cow we butchered every fall, dozens of chickens, and more home baking than we could ever consume.

Eating food—lots of it—was important to us. We took the saying "Eat, drink, and be merry, for tomorrow we may die" literally. We had piles of meat, often two or three kinds, at every meal. A typical breakfast was fried eggs and jreewe, or cracklings, little bits of bacon stored in pig fat.

And for breakfast dessert—yes, breakfast dessert—we ate fresh homemade bread dipped in thick cream with several tablespoons of sugar mixed in. Sometimes we skipped the main course and just ate dessert. Making a perfect start to our day were halva, a sweet, sesame-based fudge, with fresh buns, a favorite from Ukraine, and Napoleon torte, a dozen crispy, cake-batter crepes, layered with thick, creamy vanilla pudding and left to soak overnight.

As Mom would say, "Eat, eat; who knows what tomorrow might bring?"

An Act of Building Community

Jake Tilitzky, the profoundly humble, simple, and deeply spiritual pastor of our church, dedicated his life to us. Even in his eighties, he is still presiding over funerals (including my parents', several years ago). He had experienced the same terror of war and famine but somehow was able to rise above the fear and help us bear the burden and make sense of the senseless horror of it all. His sermons were filled with stories of our past. As I remember, he acknowledged the pain we had experienced but placed it in the context of God's will for our lives. Even for those who doubted a God who would allow so much pain and death, his words offered deep comfort, an important lifeline to a people who otherwise might have experienced mass insanity.

Several times a year, Jake stood at the pulpit and prepared us to take Communion two Sundays hence. He was aware of the toll that fear can take on a people: of the mistrust, unresolved anger, and mental anguish that could tear us apart. Communion, under Jake's leadership, was a time for each of us to reconcile not only with God but also with one another.

Though he was a short, balding man, to a child sitting in the front row, as was the custom in our church, Jake grew larger in the pulpit during his sermon when he spoke the words "In two weeks' time, we will be taking Communion"—the way he said this indicated that the practice was not optional—"and should there be anyone in this congregation who is not right with someone in the congregation, I encourage you to reconcile. He that is not right with another cannot be right with God." If you were so much as angry with another person in the congregation, you could not take Communion. And if you did not show up for Communion, it would be only a matter of days before Jake would show up at your home and ask if there was anything you wanted to tell him.

Shortly after we arrived home from church on the Sundays when that sermon had been preached, my dad would start pacing around our house. My parents, as they began to make more money from farming, also bought and sold farms and houses as investments. At times these properties were bought from or sold to others in the congregation. More often than not, some mistrust and friction surfaced, rising from our shared trauma.

So my dad would pace. At first he would deny that anything was wrong or that he was to blame. If he had done something wrong, he would say, it was up to the person wronged to call. Mom and all of us kids knew to hang low and wait it out. And sure enough, several hours before Communion, my father would pick up the phone and make the call, dissipating the tension and angst in our home. He had chosen joy over fear.

This simple act of building community and choosing joy over fear gave us a distinct advantage. We were team players in a society that was organized on the basis of individualism. We needed less and could do more. Most important, we learned very quickly and shared what we knew with one another, whether improved farming techniques or how to buy and sell land or where to get the best deal, a key advantage in our business affairs.

As I grew up, I never questioned why we might work for a better world together. My sense was that what we were doing for Mennonite Central Committee, a worldwide relief agency, we did because it had helped us in our time of need and now we wanted to give back. Whenever we made soap or quilts, or sent care packages or money, something inside me was renewed.

I often wonder if the only way we can ever really transcend the collective evil we endure as people is to do good together. Maybe loving our enemy and repaying harm with good is the only way to achieve true healing—and, in turn, joy.

The Mennonite Turn

My community's definition of itself based on fear ended up being largely positive. Why did that happen? How did that happen? Are there insights for us as we try to understand how we can deepen community?

You could call this transformation in the community of my youth "the Mennonite turn." Fear usually begets more fear. While we could have let fear destroy us, we turned away from it and helped those inside and outside our community who were consumed by it. Our pacifist faith taught us that lashing out was not an option, which meant that all we had left was to make things better—at first for ourselves, but then for others too.

Think about this in our times of high unemployment and underemployment: I never knew a person in our church to lack work or go hungry. We were well organized collectively to prevent this from happening. Helping one another was recognized not so much as "doing good" as expressing our solidarity with those who were in need. Funerals and weddings were catered by the women in our church, which brought the cost of the massive gatherings down to only dollars per person. Whenever there was a need, someone stepped up and helped out the best they could. Creating intentional ways to support one another and to show that we cared for the other was critical to the health of our community. It was more than the right thing to do; it was just what you did. We had experienced so much hardship as a people that we decided, collectively, not to allow such hardship again.

Fear also led us to reach out to others beyond our community. Many Mennonites from Ukraine had been helped by Mennonite Central Committee, an organization formed in the 1920s to address turmoil and famine after the Russian Revolution. This organization grew to help many Mennonites to move from Russia to Canada, Paraguay, and the United States. MCC had helped most, if not all, of the members of our church.

Our congregation donated money to MCC's work overseas through such fundraising events as the annual Mennonite Relief Sale, for which we made massive kettles of borscht and fresh-baked goods (my mother's buns always sold out before the official start of the sale). Women in the church spent the entire winter quilting and making care packages, and families got together to make soap.

The collective nature of giving back was an important part of our healing process as a people. I often think of the alternatives. One might have been to do nothing. We were all poor and tired and in need of healing, so our attitude could have been to let someone else do the good work. Another might have been to lash out or get revenge or justice for what had happened to us, investing resources to get even and feel vindicated. A third alternative might have been to invest in memorializing our plight and making heroes of the victims.

We chose instead to invest in helping those who were still suffering, whether they be our own people or others who were refugees from famine and war. Our conviction came not just from our biblical understanding of service but also from our own need to make sense of the atrocities that had been committed against us. We chose to interpret this as an awakening and a calling to help those who were now suffering the fate we once endured. I believe that this was a form of collective healing.

What Are We Afraid Of?

What is the fear that resides in many of us today? What can we learn from those who have been afraid and acted as communities in terrible ways? What can we learn from those who acted differently, who overcame fear and hatred to live peacefully? Can we learn to work together, to bind ourselves together in communities that do good for one another?

As global climate change ravages the world as we know it, will we work together to help one another, or will we build walls to keep those most affected away? Will we wage war to obtain lands that are least affected? Will the desperate among us wage war against those we believe to be holding us down?

Will Africa—the continent that has contributed the least to the environmental crisis but is suffering the greatest effects—rise up against the West? What if those whose lands are drained dry by drought and whose cities are destroyed by increasingly powerful storms decide that protecting themselves means eliminating those who continue to pollute and consume vast amounts of the world's resources?

What about terrorism? After 9/11, we were led to believe that anyone and everyone is suspect. Were those men who got into planes, hijacked them, and crashed them into buildings not ordinary people living next to ordinary people before they did this? I must admit, every time I flew during the following year, I found myself observing those who looked like the terrorists we saw on TV.

Fear can pull us apart, or it can bind us together. It can cause hatred and genocide, or reflection and altruism. Fear is a huge motivator for community. It can bring people together to destroy others or to make the world a better place. Both expressions of fear, both responses to fear, are community. We will need to choose. We have a choice. In these times we would be wise to stay together, take care of one another, and work together for a better world.

The Challenge

What I have shared is a story of being defined by community. Born a Born, I was a part of the Mennonite community and all it entailed. However, very few of us today have the experience of being defined primarily by our community. Indeed, I and many others who did grow up defined by our community are faced with a decision: Do we let our longing for community past freeze us in time (if that is even possible), or do we use that experience to develop and fuel a process of defining and choosing community?

The challenge we face today is how to define community when the complexity of life means it is no longer able to define us.

Sociologists from the late nineteenth century on have documented the fragmentation of our experience of community. As Max Weber points out, for example, the move from agrarian to urban society, the departure of so many people from the faith of previous generations, our ability to travel far from the place of birth and childhood, the speed of communications, displacement because of famine or war—all these have jammed our community signals. We may long for a time when community defined us, but we must face the reality that today it must be defined by us.

Why are so many of us finding it difficult to deepen our experience of community? What do we need to do? Where do we find the energy for the effort required to deepen our experience? The questions all of us face are many: Will we throw up our hands in the face of complexity and settle for shallow community? Or will we join hands together to choose, to create, deep community? Will we allow fear to foster antagonisms that drive us away from and against one another, or will we make the turn to transcend our fear, seeking and finding joy by helping those who fear?

Some have likened the rooted, predictable, consistent experience of community in the past, when society was less complex, to sitting down with family and friends at a table and partaking together in several courses of a good meal. They say that the contemporary experience of community, in contrast, is akin to eating at a smorgasbord: we don't necessarily know the people we are eating with, and it is up to us, individually, to decide what we will eat and in what quantity.

My sense of community when I was growing up was very much like a predictable and sumptuous dinner eaten with those whom I loved and who loved me. But the times being what they are, I have had to let go of that experience, at least as something that can be attained to any significant degree.

While I will always be grateful for what I had, and will always draw on it, I believe that, today, we must make a virtue of the smorgasbord approach. Acknowledging the fragmentary nature of smorgasbord dining does not require us to make poor choices in what we eat. It is possible to choose wisely in such a venue—to fill our plates with plenty of vegetables and fruit: lots of fiber and not too much red meat. Similarly, in the process of deepening community, I may weight my experience of my faith community to the point of giving my time, resources, and presence to its efforts in its neighborhood and limit my love of baseball to attending games when the spirit moves me—not because I have season tickets.

And besides, what is to keep us from turning to the anonymous diners around us and asking them to join us? What is to keep us from turning them from strangers to neighbors? What is to keep us from surrounding them with love and, in doing so, finding deep joy together in these chaotic times?

4 Options for Deep Community

We must reinvent a future free of blinders
so that we can choose from real options.
—DAVID SUZUKI, SCIENTIST,
ENVIRONMENTALIST, AND BROADCASTER

*t*HE THREAT OF CHAOS, experienced in the depredations
of history and anticipated in a world intent on environmental
genocide; the deep sense of aloneness in the midst of community; the creation of community by various groups on the basis
of fear—these are the challenges we face when we attempt to find
community.

But surely we are like children who refuse to eat their meal
because all they want is dessert. Surely it is laughable for us to
long for community in the midst of such plenty. Many of us are
surrounded on every side by loving family members and friends,
a peaceful and law-abiding society, a faith community.

I think that it is not immature for us to feel this way. The
irony of globalization is that what it giveth—a sense that we are
part of a wonderfully diverse macro community—it taketh away:
the reality of being part of a vibrant local, micro community. As
mentioned at the close of the previous chapter, it seems that in our

hyped-up, sped-up, technology-driven world, the onus is on us, as individuals, together, to define community, to choose community, to make community. The reality of our time is that community is situational. It changes at different stages of our lives. I might be very active in a spiritual community and have a tremendous sense of belonging, but then, after some time, that changes. In what admittedly may be a coping system, I feel a sense of comfort in knowing that I do not need to hold on to one community or even to consider one community my primary community. Many experiences of community are possible, and I can engage in many at the same time.

A Contemporary Take on Community

In light of this, I have developed, in my work as a community activist and writer on community, a contemporary take on community. In my research into the concept of community—an exciting though somewhat perplexing process, for the literature is rich and the definitions many—I have settled on five broad categories that I believe capture the basic understandings of community, these being important for us to consider as we explore the possibility of deepening community today:

- Community as identity
- Community as place
- Community as spiritual
- Community as intentional
- Community as a natural living system

Community *as* Identity

The most basic understanding of community is our use of the term to identify ourselves.

"My community." These two simple words can say so much about a person. They can tell us where a person comes from and the context in which their beliefs and aspirations were shaped. They can give us insight into the person's friends and connections, family, and lifestyle.

Ubuntu is a widely used African term. It is rich in meaning, describing the interconnection between people: "I am human because I belong." Being human is defined as individual and social but precisely as belonging to one another. In his book *No Future Without Forgiveness*, Archbishop Desmond Tutu describes the concept of ubuntu this way: "My humanity is caught up, is inextricably bound up, in yours." We belong in a bundle of life; a person is a person through other persons. If I am accomplished, it is not the "I" who identifies the accomplishment but the "we." We gain our identity and sense of purpose in the context of our community. I like this definition a lot because it describes the interconnectedness not only of our identity but also of our actions.

Family is another primary source of community identification. To identify oneself as being from a particular family provides a context of relationships. In some cultures, descending from a particular family spanning many generations brings status—sometimes high status and sometimes low. Being part of an extended family can be a powerful source of community identity.

So can association with a cause, particularly if the cause provides a sense of solidarity and brings feelings of belonging. Communities of association are most often formed by those who feel outside, or on the margins of, the mainstream and who are struggling together for broader acceptance in society.

One example is the gay community, in which people who have suffered discrimination because of their sexual orientation have bonded to advocate for change. This identity often goes beyond advocating for a cause, resulting in gay people living close to one another and establishing places for social contact and the expression of their faith. Two other important examples of identity as community are the disability community, which often is composed of parents campaigning for a safer and more inclusive society for their children, and the feminist community, a blend of women who campaign for equality.

Communities by association can cross many boundaries. Most often they are not restricted by geography; rather, they provide a context for identifying with others like oneself or with a cause about which one cares deeply. In turn, they provide a gateway to deepen one's experience of community.

Community as Place

Place may be more important to some of us than others, but we all live somewhere and with others around us. Indeed, the most common use of the term community is as a description of place: the community where I live—my home, neighborhood, city, or village. The writers I read most often—community developers, economists, and people concerned with social policy—are concerned with improving the condition of place in order to deepen community. They talk about community as place in the contexts of community building, community design (of neighborhoods), and social networks.

Community building describes the betterment of a community through improving its physical conditions—for example, by restoring historic buildings or renewing neglected neighborhoods. It also refers to the process of building a community's social infrastructure by improving the skills that citizens need for participation and opportunities in which to participate. The goal is to create conditions for citizen engagement and empowerment, helping them to agree on what needs to be improved, to feel that they have the power to make the changes, and to be willing to work at doing so.

Community *design* can have an impact on the cohesiveness and effectivenes of community life, facilitating it or hindering it. The Italian piazza, or civic square, facilitates coming together and relating. In contrast, houses built with double-door garages facing the street obstruct people from connecting naturally with one another. Neighborhood pubs and coffee shops can become places where neighbors meet naturally; not so when they are placed in areas where roads are designed to move cars quickly through a place without consideration of pedestrian activity. The proximity of people can greatly enhance opportunities for connecting frequently and meaningfully. The social conditions of neighborhoods play a large part in determining quality of life. Think of the levels of mistrust and fear that exist in neighborhoods with high levels of crime.

The goal of designing walkable communities is to facilitate connection by making it more a part of everyday life—for example, meeting a neighbor while walking to the grocery store.

Possibly the most defining aspect of community as place is the cohesiveness of the people who live there, what is often referred to as social capital. The term is most commonly identified with Robert Putnam, whose work focuses on the importance of social networks, norms of reciprocity, mutual assistance, and trustworthiness among citizens. In *Better Together: Restoring the American Community* and other publications, Putnam is particularly concerned with the loss of social capital in U.S. communities and what might be done to rebuild it.

Social networks are the way we get to know one another better over time. The more we connect, the better off we are. Putnam describes two kinds of social networks. The first and more common kind is created by bonding with people who are like us. I am a Mennonite and therefore find commonality and comfort in the company of other Mennonites. The second, equally important kind involves bridging by connecting and engaging with people who are not like us—people who have different belief systems or skin color or socioeconomic status. I am heterosexual but am part of a church that welcomes loving people from multiple sexual orientations. Though we are different, we can bridge these differences and build cohesiveness.

Community *as* Spiritual

Religion may be in decline, but spiritual practice and the search for truth and understanding continue to draw people together. Spiritual practice defines community for many of us, whether it takes place in churches, mosques, synagogues, ashrams, temples, or small groups of spiritually motivated people meeting together in retreats or in their homes.

For many of us, gathering for worship and prayer defines our most profound experience of regular community. In our place of worship, we experience connection to our faith and the people who share our faith. This physical place of gathering becomes a tremendous source of personal and community identity.

A community of faith helps people to strengthen their spiritual understanding and discipline their spiritual practice. A sorting of ideas, both supportive and challenging of lifestyle, reaffirms the importance of a common bond and understanding. The community seeks to forge conformity of experience and belief.

Healthy spiritual practice, however, allows for "creative seeking" and for challenging belief, both personal and collective. This helps the community to grow in understanding and strengthens the overall belief system. Being in spiritual community is often cited as the essential ingredient in deepening spiritual practice.

"I am Muslim," or Christian, Mormon, or Buddhist, is a way not only to express a personal belief system but also to indicate an important source of identity. The statement creates the expectation of behavior in keeping with the belief system of the group. "As a Muslim, I practice Ramadan and eat halal meat." "As a Christian, I have been baptized, and I celebrate Christmas and Easter."

There is more. Christians identify themselves as Roman Catholic or Protestant or Eastern Orthodox — and, in the case of Protestants, even more narrowly as Presbyterians or Anabaptists or members of other denominations. Muslims identify themselves as Sunni, Shia, Hanafi, Shafi'i, Maliki, or Humbali. All are Muslim, but the name by which they are known and wish to be known identifies their understandings or traditions within that faith. When people name their faith tradition, they share not only their belief system but also their chosen community of faith. This can forge community in both positive and negative ways, as we have seen in some fundamentalist denominations where faith causes blind choices. Spiritual community, when open, can help us to deepen our commitment to each other and, in turn, be a wonderful place for joy together.

Community *as* Intentional

The ideal of community as a way of life, or as the fulfillment of an idea or vision, has led to the formation of intentional communities, which I see as the fourth broad understanding of community.

Most often these are physical communities—for example, kib-
butzes, ashrams, monasteries, communes, and housing cooperatives—in which people make a long-term commitment to live
together in significant cooperation. In some intentional communities, people share everything, including finances.

Intentional communities may be set up for their members
to live according to specific spiritual ideals, or to perform acts of
service—for example, on behalf of the disabled, the imprisoned,
or refugees—or to support a social or political ideal.

The definition of intentional community may be broadened by
including retreats or short-term service projects in which people
gather to experience community and then take the experience into
their everyday lives with an enhanced commitment to community.
The work of the late M. Scott Peck is particularly significant in
this area. He and his colleagues developed Rabata Retreats, believing that "love is the will to extend one's self for the purpose
of one's own or another's spiritual growth." The retreats, which
continue, move participants through a variety of teachings and
stages of learning, leading them to experience the formation of
community within just a few days.

Another compelling example is Jean Vanier's L'Arche movement, which brings dignity to people with developmental disabilities. This movement began with communities in France and
has spread all over the world. Though there are many long-term
L'Arche members, most come as assistants to live with the handi-
capped for a few months to a few years. They take into their everyday life the profound sense of belonging that they experience
through L'Arche.

By forming an intentional community, people employ a deliberate set of actions to build a sense of community. The intent
is to undertake strategies that will deepen bonds between people.

An example may be someone moving into a neighborhood and creating experiences to deepen relationships between neighbors. Such people are intentional about their desire for community and focus their energy accordingly.

Community as a Natural Living System

An understanding of physics and biology has contributed to our understanding of community. My favorite writers in this area are physicists Fritjof Capra and David Bohm and leadership expert Margaret Wheatley. These and others use science's understanding of the interrelationships of all things to deepen our understanding of community.

We are one big community in that all matter and all organisms are interconnected. Community is the way all living things are organized. As Capra writes in *The Hidden Connections: A Science for Sustainable Living*, "At all levels of life—from the metabolic networks inside cells to the food webs of ecosystems and networks of communications in human societies—the components of living systems are interlinked in network fashion."

David Bohm calls this an "unbroken wholeness," a concept he discusses throughout his book *Wholeness and the Implicate Order*, suggesting that events that are separated in space and are without possibility of connection through interaction are nonetheless correlated in ways that defy casual explanation—meaning that everything we do affects everything else. We are connected both physically and metaphysically.

And in *Finding Our Way: Leadership for an Uncertain Future*, Margaret Wheatley writes, "The instinct of community is not peculiar to humans but is found everywhere in life, from microbes to the most complex species."

All around us are webs of connection. Each connection evolves through interaction, ultimately creating a harmony among the whole.

The Essence of Community: Belonging

Some people have shared with me that the only way we can talk about community effectively is to agree on a common definition. I am not of that school. *Community* is one of those words that have many meanings, primarily because the experience of community is so diverse and rich. Words are not always the best way to describe such complex experiences. Like the words *love* and *fear*, *community* has many meanings that change based on context or circumstance.

That said, I believe that there is a word that gets at the essence of all these different understandings, and that word is *belonging*. A sense of "knowing that I belong" is the most common desire of those who wish to build community, but it is also one of the least realized desires. Belonging is experienced when acts of mutual caring are frequent and when personal identity is associated with the group.

Belonging means to feel that we are in the right place, to be made to feel welcome in a place or a group. It is to be cared for and to reciprocate that caring, to know that "I am home." It is a willingness to extend our identity to a people or experience.

Family is the most common source of belonging. Family members share a common history and bond, and family is a natural place for mutual acts of caring to occur. Identity forged during childhood is strongly influenced by family. But family is less important to some people than others—more negative than positive for a few—and it may provide less a sense of belonging today than in the past, as people often live a long way from one another.

Places of worship, service clubs, and community centers, which create trusting communities over time, can provide an environment of belonging that provokes mutual acts of caring. Helping one another during illness, supporting one another through celebrations and tragedies, knowing what is going on in one another's lives, and caring and acting collectively are all part of communities of belonging.

Belonging can be achieved in certain types of workplaces, especially when a group's work and the sense of purpose of its members merge. In the early days of Greenpeace and religious charities such as the Catholic Social Movement and Mennonite Central Committee, merged purpose created feelings of belonging among members. Corporations such as Disney, Apple, and Ben & Jerry's have created internal cultures committed to corporate social responsibility.

Close friends and neighbors, over time and through many experiences, can form bonds of belonging that are not easily broken by a change in circumstance or a move to another city. The cultural bonding among immigrants provides a sense of connection and promotes acts of mutual caring, creating a community of belonging in a new country.

Five Simple Principles of Community

I am not proposing a simple understanding of community or even an easy one. Rather, I am appealing for a broader definition of community as belonging, a definition that allows us to embrace community as it is, when it is. Rather than wasting time and energy protesting the fragmentation of our lives today, and rather than using fragmentation as an excuse to withdraw and look after number one, we can choose to make a virtue of this multiplicity of community experiences.

I have found that my "community anxiety" is quelled and my longing for community is met through understanding five principles of community:

- Seeking community is natural.

- We all have many communities in our lives.

- We can choose to deepen our experience of community.

- Seeking community is part of our spiritual journey.

- Healthy community leads to individual and collective altruism.

Seeking Community Is Natural

As living organisms, we gravitate toward one another. Something deep inside us knows that together we are more. We can accomplish more together, we are safer together, and we can find greater comfort when we are together. We all know community when we see it or feel it. Being in community is our natural state.

We All Have Many Communities in Our Lives

Community is not something some people have and others do not. We all have community in our lives. As discussed above, communities can be where we live or among people with whom we socialize, play, or work. They can be composed of family, neighbors, gang members, people with whom we worship or commit crimes. Not all communities are equal, nor are all communities healthy. Community is therefore not an ideal state; it just is.

We Can Choose to Deepen Our Experience of Community

The best judge of a healthy community is the individual in community. We have choices: to join a community, to stay in a community, to leave a community, to contribute to a community, and, most important, to identify with a community. The extent to which our personal identity becomes part of the collective identity is up to us.

The function of a community is unique to those who join it. The more important the function of a community in their life, the deeper their commitment. We can choose to connect and become involved; we can choose to be committed and to express belonging. We can even choose to be fully engaged and allow our identity to merge with the identities of others. In every community of which we are a part, we have chosen the function it plays in our lives.

Let us look at the notions of shallow and deep community a bit further. To think of something as shallow versus deep is a form of judgment. I am swimming in shallow water and I want deeper water. I want a deep conversation and this one is so shallow. The journey from shallow to deep is driven by a desire for more. It defines the search for more community, better community. It counters fragmentation by demanding deeper relationships and experiences.

Another way to consider shallow versus deep, however, is to take the judgment out—to consider shallowness or depth purely as an observation, and to see one as not necessarily better than the other but as a choice we make.

- "I am so glad this is a light movie; I am not sure I could handle a deep one tonight."

- It is good to feel alone sometimes, as in, "I want to be alone right now."

By observing community as deep versus shallow, we may be expressing a longing or just making an observation. Perhaps we do not want a deeper connection with work colleagues, but we do want to get to know our neighbors better. Our choices may be difficult or may be situational, but they are our choices, and so the outcomes are of our own making.

Seeking Community Is Part of Our Spiritual Journey

Seeking meaning in life; finding purpose, understanding, and pleasure—these things that engage our souls and enliven our spirits also provide the context for connection and community. In the pursuit of a meaningful life, we engage with others. We seek those with whom we identify, who enjoy what we enjoy, whose purpose is similar to ours, who validate our search. This does not mean that we seek only those who are like us—though by default that is the easiest thing to do. Rather, it means that we seek people who are engaged by the things that engage us.

Healthy Community Leads to Individual and Collective Altruism

When we find one another, are engaged together, and realize that our personal identities are becoming associated with the identity of the community, we naturally reach out to one another. Individual acts of altruism create norms of behavior and can become acts of collective altruism that benefit all.

The paradox of collective altruism is that we receive personal benefit by acting for the good of the whole. We are willing to suspend personal need in order to contribute to collective need, knowing that our personal experience of community will be enhanced. In this way, belonging is strengthened.

Many healthy communities, having experienced the joy of collective altruism, reach out beyond their identified community to share the joy with others. In turn, the collective is strengthened.

The Continuum of Community Experience

We have come to a point where we may say that finding and building community is a series of experiences and choices that evoke a feeling of connectedness or togetherness—of belonging—in which we are invited to become more and more engaged. I have reorganized the matrix that we looked at earlier (see chapter 2) in order to depict the differences between no community, shallow community, fear-based community, and deep community in light of the four main acts of building community that I have identified (listed in the first column). I have also added a final element (see the bottom of the first column), "Giving your full identity," to indicate the intentionality of people at different points on the continuum.

I do not mean to suggest that everyone starts at "no community" and must work their way through each type of community experience to get to deep community. The starting point for some will be no community or shallow community; for others it will be fear-based community; for still others it may even be deep community. The move from no community to shallow community is not that difficult. However, the two experiences are often confused with each other. For example, what we call shallow community may actually be no community: experiences that are entertaining or fulfilling to individuals—at most a form of collective individualism. To move from fear-based community to deep community most likely will require us to transcend our natural

COMMUNITY BUILDING	NO COMMUNITY	SHALLOW COMMUNITY	FEAR-BASED COMMUNITY	DEEP COMMUNITY
Share your story.	This is my story.	Entertained, no emotional bond.	I am not one of them.	To open doors between us. Stories unite us.
Enjoy one another.	What's in it for me?	Time-limited connection.	Join against others. We must stop them.	Shared identity. This draws us together. Seeking deeper connection.
Care for one another. (Build social capital.)	Hedonism	Friends we see once a month, family at Christmas. We have association but lack bonding.	Bond together against others or something. We are right and they are wrong.	Knowing one another by repeatedly spending time together. Mutual acts of caring build a sense of belonging.
Take care of one another. (Empathy and belonging.)	Take care of yourself— no one else will.	Send a get-well card, phone on their birthday, Facebook birthday post. Our doctor cares for us when we are sick.	Believe that "we" have a greater right to life (happiness) than "they" do. We are stronger when they are weaker.	Celebrate together in person, children know and trust us, we know and act when neighbors and friends and family members are sick, mutual acts of caring occur often.

COMMUNITY BUILDING	NO COMMUNITY	SHALLOW COMMUNITY	FEAR-BASED COMMUNITY	DEEP · COMMUNITY
Work together for a better world. *(Collective altruism.)*	I am alone in this world.	Send in a donation, click "Like" on Facebook, sponsor a child in Africa yet do not know names of children next door.	Share a belief that we are right and they are wrong; work together to realize that belief. If we work together, we can win and they will lose.	Share a belief that creates a benefit for all; act together for the benefit of all. An absence of "they" or "them." As we care for others, our caring for each other deepens.
Giving your full identity.	Delusional.	Born into this community. These are my people.	I will do whatever it takes for my "tribe" or people to win and defeat the other.	I believe in this so much that I will give my whole self to this.

desires and responses, as in the case of my own community, a process that I described in chapter 3 as the "Mennonite turn."

Whenever we are together with other people, belonging can emerge. Our focus must be on the four simple but important acts that have proven to deepen community both individually and together. Beginning with the next chapter, I devote a chapter to each one of these.

Sharing Our Stories

The first is sharing our stories (chapter 5). Sometimes we tell these just to ourselves, to invoke memory of community, but better yet, we share our stories with others. Sharing stories deepens community because through this activity we open ourselves to one another, show our vulnerability, and build mutual trust.

Enjoying One Another

The second act of deepening community is simply learning to enjoy one another, even engaging in play when we get together with others, and then doing this consistently over time with the same people (chapter 6). It may sound too good to be true, but enjoying one another is at the root of deep community. This can mean playing games or music, or watching movies together. It can mean worshipping, volunteering, or working together—just about anything that brings us joy and that we do on a regular basis with the same people.

When we play on a regular basis with the same people, we build social bonds, increase our capacity to learn from others, and strengthen what is commonly referred to as our "emotional intelligence." In a relaxed manner, we enjoy the company of others, make mistakes, pick up cues, and learn to be together. When we enjoy one another, we create positive memories and associations. When we enjoy one another's company, we want to spend more time together, and this strengthens our sense of belonging.

Caring for One Another

The third act is being intentional about being cared for and taking care of one another (chapter 7).

We are empathic creatures with a deeply held instinct for compassion, feeling one another's joys and pain. Helping one another: this is key to the survival (and evolution) of all living things.

For homeowners, this may mean joining a neighborhood watch or a block parent program. For parents, it may mean belonging to a co-op to share child care with other parents. At work, it may mean remembering birthdays and special holidays together, having parties, or just taking the time to hear coworkers' joys and needs. For siblings, it may mean bringing soup over when a brother or sister is sick, caring for an elderly parent, or just listening to one another.

Working Together to Build a Better World

The fourth act of deepening community is committing to work with others (preferably the same people over time) for a better world (chapter 8). This may mean improving a neighborhood near our work or church. It may mean retrofitting our building to be more environmentally sustainable. It may mean starting a recycling program in our neighborhood or, if we have one already, carrying our recycling to a centralized place with ten other households so that the truck idles less. It may mean cleaning up a park, feeding the hungry, or visiting prisoners together.

When we do these things as individuals, we are able to express our altruism. When we do these together, with collaborative intention, we create the power of collective altruism. Something special happens when we are part of an ongoing group of caring. We not only do good for others but also, through our collective energy, experience a strengthened bond with one another.

There are other ways to build connection, but these four simple acts—sharing our stories, enjoying one another, caring for one another, and working together for a better world—are, in my experience, the most powerful. Each is compelling, but—as I have seen again and again, to my great joy—when all four are present in our interactions and connections, that is when we can experience the full benefits of community.

5 Sharing Our Stories

It's like everyone tells a story about themselves inside their own head. Always. All the time. That story makes you what you are. We build ourselves out of that story.

—PATRICK ROTHFUSS, AMERICAN FANTASY WRITER

*t*HIS CHAPTER PRESENTS stories of people I know: people of various ages and backgrounds, all of them finding, creating, and deepening community in ways that nurture and sustain their lives and the lives of others. They do so by creating their story of community and sharing that story with others. Perhaps you will identify with them. Or they may remind you of a neighbor, friend, or family member. I offer their stories as a reminder that we are all seeking together and that community comes in many forms. What is your story?

I travel a lot to share my story of community and to encourage people to share their stories—often with complete strangers. My good friend Peter Block, author of *Community: The Structure of Belonging* and other books, has taught me to ask participants a specific, compelling question at the beginning of my presentations and workshops. As each person present considers that question—

"Why is it important that I am here today?"—we are able to share our intent for our time together. I have found this to open us up to ask questions and become curious about one another as fellow travelers in the search for community.

Another question I often have participants ask one another in small groups is, "Who are you, and what brings you to this work?" This question invites inquiry and at the same time allows us to share our broader story—our history and, for many, our purpose in life.

Yet another question is to ask people for their first memory, or most meaningful experience, of community. I am amazed how much easier it is for us to become vulnerable (a wee bit) when we hear the story of another first.

The stories that follow come out of just such an exercise. Most are stories of people I know well. I have chosen them because they represent everyday situations in which they have struggled to find community and, in turn, deepened their experience with others. In the case of several of the stories, I have changed the name by request, and at least one of the stories is a composite of what I heard from interviews with several people I know. I encourage you to pick a story that resonates with you and use it as an inspiration to share your own story and longing, either in your journal or, better yet, with a friend or family member.

At the end of each story, I relate some of my observations or those shared with me during the interview in which I received the story. These observations provide what I consider wisdom moments and teachings for us to use on our own journeys toward deep community.

At the end of this chapter, I build on these stories to discuss some of the key benefits of community for our everyday life.

ANITA'S STORY   *Seeking a Bond in a Disconnected World*

Anita is in her early thirties and the mother of two young children. Life can be hectic taking care of little ones, yet Anita also works part-time, is active in her church, and volunteers when she can. Her story reflects the role that a mothers' group plays in supporting her and giving her a deeper experience of community.

Bonded by their faith and the experience of giving birth during the spring and summer of the same year, Anita and the core members of this mothers' group have been meeting once a week for six years. Together, they have built a sense of community around their own stories—of pregnancy and childbirth and child care and family. They meet in one another's homes, with the children playing while the moms visit (when they're not mediating disputes, that is).

These women have supported one another through subsequent pregnancies and an adoption, helped with moves and illnesses, and been sounding boards for those experiencing the frustrations that can arise with children, schools, and quirky family dynamics. Twice a year, these moms make a point of getting together as families to try to keep the connection alive between their older children, who are now in school, and to connect dads to the group as well.

This group has been meaningful to Anita for the history she shares with its members, the fun they have together, and her knowledge that if she has a worry or concern, she can bring it to the group. What this group is missing for Anita, however, is a sense of purpose beyond itself.

"We drink tea and visit," she says, "but typically we don't delve into deeper subjects such as world issues, AIDS, or local poverty."

Anita is curious to see what will happen to the group as the children grow up and the need for a playgroup disappears. She has a feeling that most of the mothers will be looking for employment once their children are in school and that the group may evolve into a once-a-month supper club.

"Only time will tell whether our years of weekly visits will be enough glue to keep us connected when our children no longer connect us," she says.

In a sense, Anita's story of the mothers' group prepared her for a new, though related, story. The women in the group supported Anita when she and her husband adopted a daughter from China and entered into yet another community, one that formed when she and twelve other couples were thrown together as they headed overseas as part of the adoption process. They traveled together and shared the momentous experience of receiving their new children. Although geographically spread out once they returned home, these families have committed to getting together annually for a weekend to celebrate the anniversary of the adoptions.

Anita experiences deep connections as the babies in this second community grow and develop. She hopes that the girls will be able to maintain some form of connection to one another and their shared history as they mature. The adoption also introduced her to a community in her own city of families with children adopted from China and Korea. She and her family get together with these families to celebrate Chinese New Year and the Moon Festival and to participate in monthly events.

Finding a sense of purpose outside the raising of children can be difficult for a young mother, but Anita volunteers as she can. Immediately after the Asian tsunami in December 2004, she called a local development office where she had done some volunteering in the past and asked if there was anything she could do to help. They promptly put her to work answering the phone, which was ringing off the hook with people wanting to make donations. Anita was exhausted by the end of the day, but she recognized how much her presence had helped, which made the work worthwhile for her. She was grateful to be connected to people who were committed to a good cause together.

Sharing her story with other mothers was the start for Anita. Now her storytelling partners span her community and the world.

Anita's wisdom for deepening community:

- Community can be found in everyday interactions.

- The storyline of life passages—such as becoming a mother—can become the basis of community.

- Shared challenges—and adversity—can bring people together.

- A sense of comfort and familiarity leads to a feeling of community.

- Sharing experiences can be a springboard for working together for a common purpose.

LUCAS'S STORY   *Facebook Friends*

Lucas is sixteen years old. He is seeking community for deeper connection and the assurance that he fits in. For Lucas, the "operating system" of community is primarily the Internet.

Lucas is likable and responsible. He is tall, handsome, and great at both school and sports. He grew up in an average home, with better-than-average experiences of community. His closest community (but not for long) is his family, with a younger brother and loving parents who both work at jobs they like. He lives in a safe neighborhood and knows his neighbors. He has attended the same church for over a decade. He goes to a great school, where most of his friends go, and has teachers who care about his welfare. He plays on several different sports teams each year.

If you were to observe Lucas's life, you might think it seems carefree. During the week, he goes to school and studies; on weekends he sleeps in, stays up late, eats whatever and whenever he wants, plays sports, and hangs out with friends. When compared with earning a living, caring for children, and maintaining a household, his life might seem like Easy Street. But Lucas is growing up and discovering his independence. Finding connection with his friends and schoolmates absorbs most of his creative energy; he is consumed with trying to fit in. What role might community play in his life?

Even though he may not describe it this way, community has always been an important part of Lucas's life. He loves going to family reunions and visiting his cousins during holidays. Even estranged family members are welcome at family gatherings, according to Lucas.

Lucas grew up with neighbors who contributed greatly to his development; he connected in wonderful ways with the neighborhood children he played with and their parents. But when he was ten, his parents got work in another town and moved the family. Though he still sees his former neighbors a couple of times a year, the bond is distant. His current neighbors have never played the same role in his life, even though he sees them often and is active in neighborhood barbecues and the like.

Church has been a mixed experience for Lucas. He goes most often without reluctance, and at times even without his parents. Sunday school is an opportunity to connect with friends, and the main service is an opportunity to catch up on homework or sleep. He likes the communal aspect of church and the consistency and stability that have been there throughout his life.

But community is taking on a different meaning for Lucas. His family story and neighborhood story are being replaced by school friends as the central influence in his life. Going to parties and hanging out at friends' homes are taking precedence over his neighborhood and church. It might seem that community is less important to Lucas now than it was in the past—that is, unless you saw his Facebook friends list.

More than two hundred strong, this list says more about his sense of community than most might imagine. Just about every member of his school's eleventh-grade class is included, as are his neighbors from childhood and his cousins, some of whom live so far away that he sees them only every three to five years.

When I think of Facebook friends, I normally think of those unknown people who hang out in cyberspace and send random e-mails to anyone who will accept them. But this is not the case with Lucas's list. He has used Facebook as a way to connect with people; judging by his list, you might say that community is more important to Lucas now than it has ever been.

At Lucas's house, the phone never rings for him, yet he always seems to know exactly what his friends are doing and even gives his parents updates on his cousins. How so? Because of the way he uses Facebook to build his network. The people in this network are now shaping his identity and giving him a sense of belonging.

Facebook allows him to arrange social events and rides to games he is playing in, and to keep abreast of all the comings and goings of the people he cares about. It helps him to remember assignments he may have missed in class and to catch up on the gossip, which is so important in learning about the rules of engagement for teenagers. By making his profile accessible only to his friends, Facebook also allows Lucas to limit his community, much the way people do by association, as in the neighborhoods in which they choose to live or the clubs they might join.

Young people can surprise us if we look at the world through their lens. Communities are so often identified with face-to-face contact. Many may not consider the cyber-world a place for building community, but young people are showing great prowess in using this world to create communities that work for them. Lucas's Facebook community looks much like my community—though mine may be best documented in my phone and e-mail list. I struggle to get to my list as often as I can, and in my busy world that means seeing people I care about less often than I would like. In Lucas's Facebook world, he can stay connected even when people are distant. Lucas is deepening community as he stays connected.

Lucas's wisdom for deepening community:

- Community happens in many ways, and when it does, you can add the new acquaintances to your Facebook account.

- It's best to open your door only to people you know, but if you let them in once, the door is always open.

- Stay connected—we are all just a click away.

- Your Facebook profile and online ramblings say more about you than the neighborhood you live in or the clothes you wear.

- Facebook means we can always connect to our community, even when we're not at home—even if we're halfway around the world.

RITA'S STORY   *How We Live Matters*

Rita lives a half-hour from the nearest city and works on her family farm. Her life is based on the rhythms of daily farm life. She has used this life as a natural template for community sharing.

Rita works seven days a week milking, tending a garden, keeping house, and raising a family. She leaves the farm every Sunday to go to church and every Monday to buy groceries. Walking to the neighbors' farms is a hike, and getting to the city is a commute, but times with friends and family and weekday church gatherings happen often, though seldom until after eight o'clock, when the evening milking is done.

There's something special about the life that Rita and her family lead. It is far more rhythmic than most I observe. The days and the seasons each have their community patterns. The days are full, but not too full to keep Rita and her family from engaging with those around them.

A central influence in Rita's life is her church community. Both Rita and her husband have taken on leadership roles in the church, and their children are active in the youth group. The church is not just a place to meet internal needs; while it is a place that builds belonging based on the sharing of its members' stories, it is also a conduit for engaging and helping others.

The men's group secures a donated field in which to plant grain every year and ships the produce overseas through the Canadian Food Grains Bank to feed those affected by famine and war. A women's group raises funds to make thousands of tea balls each year for the Mennonite Relief Sale. Another group for years has made Sunday-night dinner for the House of Friendship, a shelter for homeless men, and yet another raises funds and builds a school or church overseas every two years in an impoverished community.

This group of people exemplifies caring and giving. And they extend this caring to one another, helping out at one another's weddings and funerals, taking care of one another and even people who are not part of the church when they get sick. For months, Rita and members of the church supported a sick elderly woman who lived across the street from the church. She was known as the Cat Lady because she owned dozens of cats. When she went into the hospital, Rita was part of the crew that cleaned her house—which, as you might imagine, was a terrible, pungent mess—after hospital personnel told this woman that she could not go home unless the cats were removed and the house sanitized.

The woman died before she could move back home, but not before she had named Rita's pastor as executor of her will, for which he received some money from the estate. Not wanting to gain personally for what he considered to be an act of kindness, he used the money to buy a defibrillator for the volunteer fire department. Several months later, he had a heart attack and was the first person to benefit from it.

Rita's son also recently had a heart attack. It was an incredibly worrisome time in the life of his family. The stent that had been placed in an artery near his heart had not been working properly, and one day when he was out running at school, his heart suddenly stopped. Fortunately, his teacher knew CPR, a doctor's office was across the street from the school, and a local nurse, who had just finished a presentation to a class, was coming out of the school just in time to help. That's not all: the local ambulance happened to be driving by at just the right time, and the volunteer fire department had its defibrillator. Her son's life was saved.

But the real miracle took place during the month of his hospitalization, surgery, and recovery in a city nearly two hours away. The phone never stopped ringing at home, meals were dropped off, endless boxes of chocolates and other gifts were sent to the hospital, and some friends and family members made the long drive daily with Rita's husband and daughter to visit at the hospital after their chores were done. People even took time off work to help the family with their spring planting since Rita was staying with her recovering son. Special wishes and prayers made this difficult time so much easier.

The connection between giving and receiving is central in Rita's life. It is not a matter of indebtedness, and not even of gratitude (though there is plenty of that); it's more just, well, this is what you do. When people are in need, this is what is good and right, Rita would say: the way of community; the sense of support and belonging that makes life good and safe for all concerned.

Though Rita lives in a small rural community, she seems deeply connected to the world. In many ways her life on the farm and at church has preserved the best of the way community used to be. Though it may sound unreal to some—too warm and ideal—the story is real, as are the people who make up her remarkable community. This community has shaped and continues to shape them. It works its way into everything. For example, when people are ready to leave after a visit in Rita's home, the entire family walks them to the door and waves goodbye as they pull away.

Rita's wisdom for deepening community:

- Where you live can increase your possibilities for community.

- Community is a lifestyle—a way of being.

- It is important to commit to a group of people.

- "Do unto others as you would have them do unto you."

- Get involved and help others; this will connect you to them.

- The more you give, the more you recieve.

JILL'S STORY　*Lonely Is a Choice*

Jill is retired and has been divorced for nearly twenty years. She lives alone in a small apartment in a housing complex for seniors.

Her daughter lives nearby, but her two sons have moved across the country for work. Jill is reinventing her community; though she is lonely at times, her active lifestyle and many new friends are giving her a renewed sense of connection.

Jill spent the first twelve years of her life on a farm in a small rural village. Her parents could not make a go of it and moved to the city for work. The family visited their village every week to see cousins, attend weddings and funerals, and get together with family friends. Jill fondly remembers falling asleep in the backseat of the car with her sisters on the way home from these visits, feeling full and warm.

Jill graduated from university, married, and started teaching biology at a large high school in the city. She loved teaching and spent time with children who were struggling in school. She also coached the women's volleyball team and was active in her local community. She took a few breaks as her own children grew but continued in her teaching career.

What happened next altered Jill's community story drastically. After her children left home for university, her marriage broke down—and so did many of the friendships she and her former husband had forged as a couple. She blocked feelings of loneliness by throwing herself fully into her career, teaching for nearly a decade more. Then she sold her home and moved into the seniors' complex.

There, however, her loneliness caught up with her. For the first year in her new setting, Jill experienced what her doctor believed was depression. But she never filled the prescription he gave her; deep down, she knew that she was dealing with a normal response to being divorced, retiring from a career, and living far away from her children.

Things took a turn for the better when her daughter, now married, moved with her two children to the city where Jill lived.

This meant so much to Jill; spending time with her daughter and grandchildren gave her renewed energy. It was wonderful to have family near again, and the smiles of her grandchildren gave her strength.

Jill decided that she had done enough keeping to herself and got involved at her complex. She joined the walking club and tried a yoga class. She volunteered at the library and a new day-care center for children. Most important, she began meeting twice a week with a group of women to visit, play cards, and share meals.

This changed the way Jill thought about herself and the community she had always been a part of. She was surprised how easy it was to find community with others—because they were seeking the same.

Jill's wisdom for deepening community:

- Finding community and belonging can happen at any age.
- Family is important but not essential to community in your life.
- It's important to reach out—someone needs to initiate community.
- It helps to find a place to live where community is part of the program.

WILL'S STORY *Losing and Finding Community*

When you have experienced intentional community, going back to everyday life is hard. That is Will's story: he is seeking a community that he feels he has lost.

Will can be very serious, but he is also warm and funny. He has a deep faith. He is always seeking conversation with others, embracing people with acceptance and sharing details of his life with an openness that I seldom experience. Visiting with him is like sitting down with an urban philosopher.

Will is unique in that he has lived in intentional community most of his adult life. He formed his first such community with friends right out of university—his first experience of the deep bond of belonging and purpose that is so intense among those who live together and share everything in common.

This experience led him, when he was still in his twenties, to an intentional community in the state of Georgia, one that was drawn together around the needs of refugees and prisoners on death row. On average, five or six families form the core of this community, joined on a temporary basis by interns, volunteers, and refugee families who stay for a few weeks to learn English and other skills to help them integrate into U.S. culture.

The partners in the community share everything in common—land, houses, and finances. They sing together, pray together, and eat most of their meals together. Will found a profound sense of belonging and purpose in this community because it was committed to building a better world together. It was here that he met his wife and they raised their three children. Life was not always easy. Everyone worked hard, raised funds to support their vision, and lived close to the land. People joined the community for many reasons—such as for a simpler life or a safe place to raise their families—but only those deeply committed to the mission stayed for long periods of time.

Life in intentional community can provide so much to those seeking a deeper experience of belonging, but it also requires its members to give much of their identity and personal will to the community. This is not as large a sacrifice as it may seem because the benefits of belonging, security, and purpose most often outweigh the need for personal expression. When living in a healthy and well-functioning intentional community, members can maintain the fine balance between personal creativity and expression and the will and needs of the community as a whole, to the benefit of everyone.

Will and his wife were able to find this balance in Georgia for a long time, until fifteen years after Will joined, when they began to feel that the well-being of their children was being challenged. The community believes deeply that they should not isolate children from the outside world, that going to public school and forming friendships outside the community is important. But the schools in their district are ranked the lowest in the state. Will and his wife—both of them university educated—became concerned about the quality of education their children were receiving and the effect this would have on their chances later in life. As their children were reaching high school age, they began to feel that homeschooling would be a better choice for them and their children. The community deliberated this question for months, ultimately deciding that the significance of integration into the larger community was too important a value to change. Will and his wife chose to leave the community and move their family to Canada, where they had both grown up.

In Canada they found an exceptional school for their children and meaningful jobs. They also met others who had a similar belief in community and bought a home next to one of these couples. Though they do not live in intentional community, the two couples are committed to supporting one another. Will and his family navigated this big change well.

A happy ending to the story, one might think. But even though Will and his family integrated well into their new life, Will experienced a profound loss of community and mission. Some days he found it hard to get going in the morning. His job seemed less important and his friendships less real, and his daily interactions lacked the sense of purpose he felt so deeply when he lived in intentional community. He was frozen by the fear that he would never find true community in his new life.

This is the point when I found Will, or should I say when he found me. He had heard that I was writing a book on community and wanted to talk. Ever seeking, desperate for meaning and fulfillment, he was hoping that I might uncover something in my research to help him find the community he was longing for in his newly chosen life.

The two of us have had many conversations. Will has tried harder than anyone I know to find community. He is pleased that his children are happy and are thriving in their new schools and environment. But he still feels an emptiness, despite volunteering with refugees learning English and identifying with their sense of loss and displacement, joining two men's groups, becoming close friends with the couple who live next door, and attending a welcoming church.

Even when he worked for a charity to build what it calls supportive housing, he did not find the same sense of connection and purpose. And now, as a self-employed carpenter, he finds his work to be largely functional and aimed at earning money to support his family. The mundane needs of urban life—paying the bills, maintaining a single-family household, driving the children to their various lessons and appointments—consume so much energy. Life takes much more effort now.

In some ways Will's transition may be likened to three of Elisabeth Kübler-Ross's five stages of grief: denial, anger, and acceptance. I am happy to say that he has arrived at a place of acceptance and has found some peace with his choice. In effect, he is infusing his new life with his earlier story of intentional community. We spend many an hour talking about what we describe as "hybrid communities"—such as cohousing and neighborhood associations—which draw from the best of intentional community but are adapted for mainstream life. And Will has the best perspective of anyone I know on what is lacking in normal community versus intentional community.

Will's wisdom for deepening community:

- Healthy community creates a deep sense of personal and financial security, for both the individual and the family. In the larger society, we are most often on our own as individuals or a family unit to fend for ourselves, which can create financial insecurity, fear, and feelings of inadequacy.

- In community, meeting needs for belonging and meaning is a shared responsibility, and children have many role models as they grow up. In the larger society, it is often assumed that one person can fufill all the needs of a spouse, and parents all the needs of their children, which puts excessive pressure on marriages and families.

- Community creates a cooperative environment in which a focus on unity and the well-being of all is maintained. In the larger society, concern for individual striving produces a competitive environment that marginalizes and impoverishes many.

- In community, the sharing of material goods supports simplicity and creates interdependence. In the larger society, sharing is difficult and often impractical, so every household has its own appliances and tools and has to work long hours to afford them.

- Community conserves energy and helps the environment. In the larger society, work, church, family, and friendships are often separated and require time and energy consumption for all the commutes that are necessary to maintain connections.

- Community can help people to focus on their spiritual lives, as faith-based communities rely on trusting God and one another.

- Job satisfaction is often quite high in community because of the cooperation and sense of mission. In the larger society, a job is often a means to an end—to pay the bills and feed the family.

- Socializing is always available in community, through singing, playing games, traveling together, and so on. In the larger society, having fun often involves significant amounts of money and time.

- In community, a person becomes a generalist, open to learning and doing new tasks. In the larger society, work has for the most part become so specialized that a generalist struggles to find a place.

- In community, the weekend is an extension of the week. In the larger society, people often live for weekends.

The Benefits of Community

We can learn from sharing our stories, especially as we begin to understand the wisdom that comes from them. In fact, this sharing benefits us, individually and collectively, in at least four main ways, providing the ground for greater caring:

- Community and belonging shape our identity more broadly.
- Community builds the conditions for mutual aid and prosperity.
- We can be smarter and more effective in community.
- Community improves our health and overall well-being.

Community and Belonging Shape Our Identity More Broadly

In the stories above, Anita adopted a child and was part of community that helped her welcome that child to a new country while encouraging the child to keep a healthy identity. Lucas was just trying to grow up. Jill was trying to find herself as a single person. Will was seeking the closeness that comes from intentional community. But what about those of us who lack the level of support experienced by these four people?

In her New York Times bestselling memoir *The Glass Castle*, Jeannette Walls tells of her poverty-stricken childhood and deeply dysfunctional parents, who could be loving but often were self-centered and neglectful. Though central figures in her life, they alone did not shape the person she would become. A series of important mentors—in particular, a small-town newspaper editor who helped her to find her talent as a writer—assisted Walls in seeing beyond her immediate situation.

Fortunately, many are the examples in which men and women have stepped up to provide emotional stability to children in situations such as the one Walls found herself in.

When we have community in our lives, we can broaden the person we see ourselves to be. Belonging can shape our identity. It can determine whether we adopt unhealthy behaviors or healthy ones. It can help us to build the skills we require to interact with others in a healthy way, and it can help us to engage in and embrace a communal approach that benefits many.

Community Builds the Conditions for Mutual Aid and Prosperity

Rita relied on her community in a time of need. Will knows how important community can be to his well-being and that of his family. Anita has built a community to support her family through a major life transition.

I tap into my knowledge of Mennonite life to understand how community aids its members. Old Order Mennonites are much like the Amish. They believe that God asks them to live slower, simpler, relationship-centered lives. Often they shun all technology—cars, television, phones, computers, and the like—and refuse government support systems or insurance of any kind. They feel that their community and their faith in God are insurance enough. When there is a medical emergency, the community takes up a collection to pay the hospital bill. As is well known, when a member's barn burns down, the community comes together to construct a new one, often in a day or two. In this way they are one another's insurance. This is their definition of "mutual aid."

In wider society, as well, we know that when people know others who are willing to help them with their job search, they are unemployed a shorter time than those who do not. We know that with an economic safety net made up of family and friends, people rely on government aid less and exit poverty more quickly.

Working together, we can do so much more. For this reason, many people have joined credit unions and cooperatives or become members of labor unions. By joining with others, we have a better chance of being successful. This also allows us to support one another. The success of one becomes the success of all.

We Can Be Smarter and More Effective in Community

Lucas intuitively understands how important it is to have a network and test ideas as he is growing up. Facebook is a great tool to help him understand others and find patterns to follow. Will shares his knowledge of how a small intentional community helped thousands of refugees with relatively little money. The wisdom of the collective created these conditions. Anita traveled with twelve other families to China to pick up her daughter. These families stayed together to help raise their children and to share how to do so in a healthy way.

John Ott, a consultant and coauthor of the amazing book *The Power of Collective Wisdom: And the Trap of Collective Folly*, is a transformative human being. Recently, when sharing his story with the Tamarack Institute's learning community, he stated,

> When human beings gather in groups, a depth of awareness and insight, a transcendent knowing, becomes available to us that, if accessed, can lead to a profound action. We call this transcendent knowing "collective wisdom." This knowing is not of the mind alone. When this knowing and sense of right action emerges, it does so from deep within the individual participants, from within the collective awareness of the group, and from within the larger field that holds the group.

This collective wisdom, he went on to say, is the hope for our future in these chaotic times. Groups have the potential to be sources of extraordinary creative power, incubators of innovative ideas, and instruments of social healing.

We are smarter together, and it is by learning together and working toward what we hold in common to be true that we will be able to find the solutions we need for a more effective world. This is consistent with Darwin's thinking later in his life that survival of the fittest also means survival of the most cooperative. When the members of a species can learn together and act collectively on what they know, they are able to succeed and grow.

Community Improves Our Health and Overall Well-Being

Rita's pastor survived a heart attack because of his community. Lucas checks in with his friends on Facebook to learn about common health concerns. Jill's mental health improved because she got involved in her community. A healthy community is a massive benefit of staying together and taking care of one another.

Dean Ornish may be the most prominent heart specialist in North America. He was chosen by *Life* magazine as one of "the fifty most influential members of his generation" and by *Forbes* magazine as one of "the seven most powerful teachers in the world." His work on reversing heart disease through lifestyle changes— exercise, a low-fat vegetarian diet, and meditation and yoga for stress release—has transformed how health professionals around the world are combating the leading killer of our time.

In addition to these three changes, Ornish observed that patients with heart disease who had a greater number of significant relationships in their lives lived longer than those who did not. This caused him to do extensive research, which resulted in his writing the book *Love and Survival: The Scientific Basis for the Healing Power of Intimacy*, in which he asserts that "perhaps the most powerful intervention . . . is the healing power of love and intimacy, and the emotional and spiritual transformation that often results from these."

The medicine that Ornish prescribes is community. "When we gather together to tell and listen to each other's stories," he writes, "the sense of community and the recognition of shared experiences can be profoundly healing."

The heart specialist quotes many research studies to back up his conclusions. People who answered no to questions about whether they had a friend who could lend them money in a difficult spot, drive them to a hospital, or care for them at home if needed had a three-to-five-times greater risk of disease and premature death from all causes.

Ornish also refers to a monograph by the renowned sociologist Emile Durkheim titled *Suicide: A Study in Sociology*, first published in 1897, which details the findings that people who were well integrated into group life, and those who were married, were far less likely to commit suicide. Ornish cites a study by David Spiegel of Stanford University showing that breast cancer survivors who engaged in a support group for a year lived on average twice as long as those who did not, as well as the finding of Dr. F. I. Fawzy at UCLA that just six weeks of support for patients with malignant melanoma were enough to boost survival times more than threefold.

Evidence shows that social ties that result in love and intimacy also help protect against infectious diseases. Dr. Sheldon Cohen at Carnegie Mellon University gave 276 healthy volunteers nasal drops containing the common-cold virus and found that individuals who had only three types of relationships—among friends, family, church, clubs, etc.—were more than four times as likely to develop a cold compared with those reporting six or more types of relationships.

One of the earliest and most significant studies recognizing the power of love and relationships, according to Ornish, was the Roseto study, which lasted nearly fifty years. In the first thirty years of the study, the population of Roseto, a homogeneous Italian-American community in Pennsylvania, had a strikingly low mortality rate from heart attacks compared with people in two adjacent towns. Roseto was settled by Italian immigrants who had strong family ties and cohesive community relationships. When the social bonds and community life dissolved among this community to the point where they were equal to those in the other towns, the incidence of heart disease rose to match the latter's rates.

Between 1979 and 1994, eight large-scale, community-based studies were conducted to examine the relationship between social isolation and death and disease. The results were remarkably consistent. Those who were socially isolated had at least two to five times the risk of premature death from all causes compared with those who had a strong sense of connection and community.

The importance of relationships and community for health and overall well-being cannot be ignored. As Ornish puts it, "We are creatures of community. Those individuals, societies, and cultures who learned to take care of each other, to love each other, and to nurture relationships with each other during the past several hundred thousand years were more likely to survive than those who did not. . . . In our culture, the idea of spending time taking care of each other and creating communities has become increasingly rare. Ignoring these ideas imperils our survival."

The good news is that the experience of community is increasingly being accepted as a better measure of wealth than the achievement of individuals and the gross domestic product (GDP) of a nation. Already, some of the world's most prominent economists are writing about the "economics of happiness." One, John Helliwell, even ends many of his talks with a children's song that includes these words:

> *The more we get together,*
> *together, together,*
> *the more we get together,*
> *the happier we'll be.*

Getting together starts when we share our stories. It gathers steam when we enjoy one another.

6 Enjoying One Another

Our most natural state is joy. It is the foundation for love,
compassion, healing, and the desire to alleviate suffering.

—DEEPAK CHOPRA, PIONEER IN THE
FIELD OF MIND-BODY MEDICINE

*W*E USE THE WORD *work* so often in connection with
community: community work, working to deepen community, working together for a better world. The word is valid, but there is something deeper behind successful community work, something that energizes the work, something that makes the work *work*, and that something is joy: the joy we feel when we are together. I feel privileged to have had an epiphany that brought all this home to me. I would like to share it with you to describe enjoying one another as the second act, after sharing our stories, of deepening community.

Ten Thousand Pies to Heal the World

It was early morning, but since it was May, the sun was already rising. I reached over to turn off my radio alarm, which was playing Johnny Cash's "Folsom Prison Blues." I got up and took a quick shower, grabbed a coffee, jumped into my car, and headed out for the half-hour ride to the village of New Hamburg, Ontario.

The Mennonite Relief Sale, which raises money for relief efforts around the world, is an annual event. Think of it as a small-town fair without the rides. A greater difference, though, is that thousands of volunteers have been working together all year, making quilts, storing fruit to make pies, and collecting items to sell on this day as a fundraiser for the less fortunate. The result is one of the largest quilt auctions in the world, a never-ending feast of homemade foods, and a series of smaller auctions that showcase everything from crafts and furniture to antique tractors.

Thousands of people, many from Toronto, descend on New Hamburg every year for this incredible event. Since its inception in 1967, the relief sale has raised more than $15 million for international development and disaster response.

When I arrived that morning at the fairgrounds, where the sale takes place, things were unusually quiet. When I checked the time on my cell phone, I realized that I must have set my alarm for the wrong time; I was an hour early for my 7 a.m. shift at the quilt auction. I had been to many of these sales and had volunteered even as a child, but I had never arrived at 6 a.m. before the crowds.

There was a quiet energy about the place as booths were being set up. I had learned as a member of the sale's board of directors for several years that no one is really in charge. Year after year, people just show up and do what they have committed to do.

On this beautiful, sunny spring day, I walked away from the grass parking lot and across a field toward an arena on the far side of the fairgrounds. To my right was a row of food stalls, where volunteers were bringing carloads of buns, meat, flour, and sugar.

Others lit fires to start the barbecues and stoves that would cook the borscht, pork-on-a-bun, apple fritters, and doughnut holes.

Past the stalls were the tents for educating people about the work of Mennonite Central Committee and the projects that the money raised that day would fund. To my left was a grandstand, where busy volunteers were setting up tables in preparation for the massive pancake-and-homemade-sausage fest that would feed thousands of early visitors. Families and friends make it a tradition to meet the last Saturday in May for these very special pancakes. The volunteers never disappoint.

Directly in front of me was the arena, where the two grand events of the fair would take place. The first was the quilt auction. Nearly three hundred quilts are auctioned every year, and some of them sell for as much as $10,000. These special ones are made by groups of women, most often in churches, and highlight special events or celebrations of landscape.

More than merely functional, the quilts are works of art. It takes more than a thousand hours, collectively, for the loving hands of dozens of expert quilters to make some of them. The painstaking work is communal and is a celebration of a faith commitment made to one another. As someone once said, "It takes a community to make a quilt; the more beautiful the community, the more beautiful the quilt." These quilts are some of the most beautiful in the world.

The same folks who auction cattle during the week (their regular jobs) volunteer on this day to sell the quilts. I am struck by the matter-of-fact way in which they sell these works of art. No emotion, no comment—just a lot number and the opening bid. This simplicity echoes the practicality of the people. The quilts may be art, but they still have a function.

My job at the relief sale was to make things easier for collectors or resellers who came from across the United States and Canada to buy the quilts. Some would leave with a dozen quilts or more. While most others were subjected to a cash-and-carry policy, they were allowed to pay for the quilts all at once after the bidding had concluded. I ensured that their quilts were safe during the auction.

Our hope was that providing special conditions to multiple-quilt buyers would drive the prices up. I seemed to have a special gift for saving prime chairs and talking up buyers as they arrived. I gave myself the unofficial title of Chief Bum Warmer.

I took great joy in knowing that the women who had spent so many loving hours creating these works of art would receive maximum return, which validated that their work was the prime attraction that day. Because of their painstaking devotion, we were raising extraordinary funds to fight famine and help victims of war and natural disasters. Many of the quilters themselves were once refugees; each of their stories was woven into the final products.

The arena was relatively empty when I arrived. The hundreds of chairs where buyers would sit were unoccupied. The quilts displayed in neat rows just outside the bidding area were attended by a smattering of serious buyers and volunteers who were prepping them and admiring the handiwork of their friends.

Just beyond the quilts were the pies. Women were already lined up in front of the left wall slicing fresh strawberries from California into bowls. These would be mixed with a sweet sauce, placed into prebaked shells, and then cut for serving—fresh, with a dollop of whipped cream. This treat is a fair favorite. Each year, thousands of pies are consumed in this way.

On the right was a booth where you could buy fruit pies to take home, though the pies hadn't arrived yet. This morning, an unusual number of young people were milling around. Some were laughing, while others were just trying to wake up. I was curious why so many were there, so early in the morning. I soon had my answer.

I heard the sound of a vehicle backing up and then the whoosh of a large truck's air brakes. An eighteen-wheel semitrailer was pulling up to the side door of the arena. It was full of pies, the work of dozens of volunteers who had gathered the day before at a commercial kitchen with huge baking ovens. My mouth dropped open. How do you make a semitrailer full of pies all by hand?

Without hesitation, one of the teenagers opened the back of the truck, jumped into it, and brought out half a dozen pies, which had been packaged in white cardboard boxes. He passed these down to a friend. Several more teenage boys jumped up into the truck and started doing the same.

Few words were shared. Obviously most of the young people had done this before, and anyone who was new fell right into line. Soon enough, a line of fifty youths reached from the truck through the back half of the arena and up into the bleachers. They passed the pies one to the other until all those white boxes reached their destination and were stacked on the bleachers, organized according to the fruit they contained.

Though it may have taken them some time to shake off their sleepiness, these young people had risen early that morning with joy and hope. They were going to meet their friends; they were going to do something important; they were going to enjoy the day together. Many of their parents joined me as I stood there watching the magical unloading of what must have been ten thousand pies.

Tears formed in my eyes. That moment—with those fifty young people unloading ten thousand pies—symbolized for me the work of the day. In that line was merged the doing of good for the world and the enjoyment of neighbors and friends. It was a place where work and play mingled nimbly, where doing what was right was amplified by the joy of doing it together. It was a celebration of community that nurtures and cares.

As I stood there with moist eyes, I felt so honored to be part of that day, to belong to this community, to have volunteered for this work that represented so much to so many. That day, through the hard work of thousands of volunteers, we raised $300,000.

I often feel that when I volunteer, I receive more than I give. This day I was given something so much more precious than the time and skills I gave. By working together with others, I received an affirmation of the person I wanted to be and the people I wanted to be with.

Four Strong Winds of Joy

In the days, weeks, and months that followed, I tried to discover the components of joy in community as I had witnessed it. I came to characterize the phenomenon as being four strong winds of joy.

The Joy of Being Together

First, I sensed the joy these young people had in being together. Yes, joy is common when young people are together, so this is not a surprising observation. What felt different was that the joy increased as the activity progressed. Knowing that they were doing something special, and that something special was happening to them, stretched their joy almost to the breaking point.

The joy radiated not only as fun but also as a deeper joy. I see and hear this same joy expressed by volunteers in organizations such as Habitat for Humanity and disaster relief organizations. It is a joy that brings a feeling of satisfaction, of knowing that you are part of a good thing.

The Joy of Collective Accomplishment

Second, there was a deep joy in the sense of collective accomplishment. Can you imagine moving thousands of pies in just over an hour and feeling so good about it? But it was even more than that.

The sense of collective accomplishment that I observed seemed similar to what we feel when playing team sports as opposed to what we feel in most of our workplaces. A collective energy built up as the work progressed, with each participant knowing the role he or she was to play. This collective energy gives energy to each individual and can draw the best out of each one. The collective action enables large-scale impact in a relatively short time, providing even more impetus and motivation. It helps us overcome the individual-level powerlessness we often feel in the face of those large-scale problems. Climate change, economic doom and gloom, and other such problems often feel overwhelming because we are so little, and nothing we individually do can change them. But we can change them by working together, especially when the energy behind our efforts is a natural, growing sense of joy.

The Joy of Collective Altruism

Third, the joy of working together for the betterment of others deepened the resolve of each person for the cause. The young people came to the work for many reasons—many of them, I am sure, were peer driven, because most of them belonged to church youth groups. There was first a shared sense of purpose.

The simplest observation is that they co-identified, or adopted, the purpose that each brought. Groups have a way of doing this when they work for, or even against, something. Psychologists call this *social identity*. People learn to identify with a group and, in turn, shape their sense of self within the context of the group. This becomes problematic only when a group identifies against another group in order to strengthen its own identity.

But this working together, when it is for the good of others (collective altruism), can create an almost metaphysical reaction that is more magical than the shared identity created by the act itself. The unloading of the pies had the feel of committed believers singing a hymn or chanting together. The collective act seemed to deepen the resolve of the many.

The Joy of Collective Lightness of Being

Fourth, working together was a powerful testament to the aphorism "Many hands make light work," which is a way of saying that when everyone gets involved in something, the work gets done quickly. I saw a deeper meaning that day in New Hamburg, that when we work together with purpose, the work feels light and the accomplishment extraordinary, resulting in joy.

Whether it is unloading pies, serving as part of a disaster relief effort, or building a Habitat for Humanity home, the work feels significant and each role feels important. The collective experience seems to transcend the reality of the work. You are not just another set of hands in a line unloading pies; you are part of an important mission to help those in need all over the world. Therefore, the work is purposeful, regardless of the task.

These are the four strong winds of joy that communities doing good, working together for the betterment of the world, generate. I liken them to strong winds because they seem to propel a people to greater action; they are the energy that is generated, providing us the opportunity to do and be more together than we can do and be alone.

Stumbling upon Joy

My dad always said that I smiled with my eyes. My hairdresser Christine makes me laugh when she says, as she trims my mustache, "Try just for a minute not to smile." I was born happy, and I consider this a true gift.

I often wonder how "my people" (Mennonites) were able to cultivate joy, given the amount of pain they had experienced and carried as refugees in a new country. The joy we felt as a family didn't come from spending a lot of money or taking big trips, which my family couldn't afford until I was a teenager. It was a great treat for us to take two hours off from chores on the farm on a hot Saturday afternoon a couple of times a year to go for a swim. I hold ridiculously wonderful memories of the times we stopped for a cold jug of A&W root beer on the way home from these swims, a rare and joyful experience for us.

Even when we were more settled and had more money and time on our hands, buying happiness was not a priority. My memories of happiness come from spending time with my extended family and going to church and helping one another. Every big event was an excuse for us to get together and eat and enjoy one another's company.

The search for happiness can be elusive, especially when we mistake it for the search for feeling good or having fun. Staying happy as I age has become a bit more difficult. I'm not sure exactly why that is; for me it just is. I would not say that I am unhappy very often (though memories of sadness are near), but I can tell that I am on a more even keel; I am more balanced about life. I still find it hard to welcome sadness, but I no longer shun it. My sense is that this is part of the journey toward wisdom.

Growing "wise" ("older" might be the more accurate word) has given me a small measure of perspective and patience. I can see the world better through the eyes of others, and this has allowed me to better feel what others feel, including sadness, confusion, fear, and, yes, happiness. Age and wisdom provide the opportunity to suspend my own observations for a while and see the world through the eyes of those with whom I come into contact. This is how I stumbled on the notion of joy and community, a theme that is sounded so well in the stories of many people I have met. I have often heard it said that what counts is not how much money you have but how you spend it. Similarly, these people are brilliant in taking what life gives them, or where life puts them, and making the most of it, not just for themselves but for the joy of many around them. A little creativity, courage, and desire can go a long way.

Mary is a good example of this. She lives in the Uptown West neighborhood of Waterloo, Ontario. As she got to know her neighbors, she learned that she lived in a unique neighborhood: one in which many people had musical skills. She had heard of porch parties and decided to take the idea to another level: she invited people to dust off their musical instruments and limber up their voices and entertain people on their front porches. As for those who were not musical, their job was to walk around the neighborhood, carrying food to share and listening to the music.

Thus was the Grand Porch Party born, which went on to attract people far beyond the immediate neighborhood. Not only did people enjoy music together, but they were able to reach out to many others and open up their neighborhood, sharing their talents with the entire community.

Sue lives on Pheasant Avenue in Cambridge, Ontario, a short street of only eight houses. She loves to cook, and, fortunately, so does just about everyone else on her street. It seemed only natural to her to bring people together through a progressive dinner. The idea is very simple: plan a four-course meal—appetizers, salad, main course, and dessert—and have four different households host one course each.

It happens several times a year on Pheasant Avenue. It takes a minimum of planning and provides a wonderful old-fashioned feeling of visiting neighbors door-to-door for special occasions. Cooking for one another, eating together—what a simple but powerful way to create joy.

The Community That Plays Together Stays Together

One way we can come to enjoy one another is by playing together. This can take as many forms as there are people. Stuart Brown, a psychiatrist and founder of the National Institute for Play, wrote the fascinating book *Play: How It Shapes the Brain, Opens the Imagination, and Invigorates the Soul.* He believes that for humans, play is innate: we are built to play. His evidence is compelling; he relates study after study showing that when we are safe and have enough to eat, humans, like all mammals throughout history, will play.

Children need play to support the phenomenal growth of their developing brains. We adults need play because it evokes optimism, gives us creative energy, reduces stress, and provides the fuel to feel pleasure. Play also helps us to develop the emotional intelligence that is essential for community, as these enjoyable activities give us the opportunity to test relationships and human behaviors with fewer consequences than more serious undertakings. Play creates a sense of belonging and binds us together. As we play, we experience common activities, emotions, and thoughts.

According to Brown, the most compelling reason to play together as a community is that play helps us to develop skills that enable us to be adaptable. By playing together, we become smarter about who we are as individuals and a collective. As playful people, we are more flexible and pliable and are better able to make sense of the changing world around us.

Understanding Joy

Joy and happiness are closely related but are different pursuits. Happiness is a feeling that most often is personal and temporal, whereas joy is a way of being. I can feel someone else's pain, or my own, and still live a life of joy. That is why, when I found the Deepak Chopra quote I used to begin this chapter—"Our most natural state is joy. It is the foundation for love, compassion, healing, and the desire to alleviate suffering"—it immediately resonated with me. Chopra's interpretation of joy rings especially true for me when I consider the role of community in nurturing a life of joy. Joy is expressed through kindness, love, and compassion, and it evokes in us altruism, caring, and the desire to end suffering. For us to grow, the joy that is in us must connect with the joy in others; giving and receiving must be mutual. Namaste, an Indian term loosely translated as "The best in me greets the best in you," may be the best foundational understanding of the life of joy.

Joy is most powerfully expressed in the desire to end suffering in oneself and others. Perhaps joy is the opposite of suffering, which is why collective altruism is such a powerful source of good. It feeds joy because as we give kindness, love, and compassion, we are also in the collective presence of joy and therefore receive the benefits of it.

Understanding the relationship between joy and happiness has been essential in my seeking (and finding) community. Happiness seems much easier to find and can be stimulated fairly easily. A piece of chocolate, a prayer, a warm coat on a cold day, a drink of whiskey to feed an addiction, or a hug from a friend—these can all bring happiness in the moment. Joy, however, comes from the way we live our lives. It is cultivated through the deep satisfaction that we are living a life of purpose and meaning with and for others. It is cultivated through showing and receiving compassion and kindness. Deep joy cannot be found alone or through individual pursuits. It can be found only in community, as we deepen our relationships with others.

This does not mean that going for a long walk by yourself or spending a week in silent meditation (two things I love to do) cannot cultivate happiness or be part of a joyful life. However, they do lack purpose and meaning in the absence of mutually caring and sustained relationships. We can cultivate joy only by giving and receiving kindness and compassion as we enter into community with others. Deepening community, therefore, is the gateway to a joyful life. And joy is the gateway into caring for one another.

7 Caring for One Another

A society can function well only if those within are concerned, not only with their own needs or the needs of those who immediately surround them, but by the needs of all, that is to say, by the common good and the family of nations.

—JEAN VANIER, FOUNDER OF L'ARCHE

WHEN MARLENE AND I were first married, we lived for five years on the ninth floor of a relatively new apartment building in Waterloo, Ontario. I am having trouble remembering even one significant conversation with a neighbor in that building. I do not recall ever having a meal with anyone.

We came and we went. There was little or no connection between us and the others who lived there. There was no green space near us, no common room within which to gather, no building association—and, even though many children lived in the building, no playground for them to enjoy. If there had been a fire at night and we were huddled outside in the dark and someone asked me, "Are the people on your floor here?" I am not sure I could have identified them.

This is a terribly sad story. Instead of benefiting from what might have been an important community-building experience, I had no sense of ownership or belonging in this community. No one there cared for me, and I did not care for them. What shocks me most, as I have listened to the thoughts and stories of many, many people, is the fact that this is not an uncommon story.

Neighbors, Proximity, and Connection

Neighbors matter, community proximity matters, connection matters. In these chaotic times, "place" matters more and more, and knowing those who live around us is increasingly important. If we see people every day, we have a far greater opportunity for community than if we simply share common interests with people spread out over the miles. When it is easy to interact with one another and enjoy one another's company, community becomes tangible and practical. We can learn from one another, observe one another, care and be cared for, and create safe places together for ourselves and our children.

Marlene and I came to this awareness partly through a vastly different experience of neighbors shortly after this, and then through the near loss of neighborliness again.

After five years of living in that apartment building, we moved a thirty-minute drive away to Pheasant Avenue in Cambridge, Ontario. The head office of the organization for which I was the executive director was located in this city, and Marlene had just entered a PhD program in Toronto. The move allowed me to be closer to my work and Marlene to her school.

We bought a real fixer-upper. We decided we would do some basic renovations for a month to get the house ready for us to move in. On our first night as homeowners, as we were stripping wallpaper from one of the bedrooms, Peter and Gary, the neighbors living in front of and next door to us, dropped in—"just to say hello, since we were out walking our dogs anyway," as Peter said. It was a simple start, but it provided the opening for us to say hello whenever we saw one another.

No one really knows why we make some connections and others not. Marlene and I had very little in common with our neighbors on Pheasant Avenue. Our interests were different, our extended communities and our careers did not overlap, and they all had dogs—we did not. The one thing we did have in common was children, and we ended up rearing them together. Because our children played together, we had many reasons to communicate. Children can indeed bond neighbors, yet I know many children-intensive neighborhoods that lack the bond of togetherness. So why did we Pheasant Avenue folk all become lifelong friends?

Proximity was a big advantage. It was easy to go on walks together, or help one another paint a deck or mow a lawn or dig a garden. We had fun together: Friday-night gin and tonics all summer long in the Staps' gazebo; swimming over at Dave and Marilyn's; Victoria Day street fireworks, garage sales, and all sorts of events during which we closed down the entire street; progressive New Year's Eve parties, with the appetizers at one house, dinner at another, and dessert and drinks at still others.

We also learned to take care of one another. We listened to work-life woes and celebrated victories. We had many birthday parties for the kids. Every year, our sons celebrated their birthday three times: a party with their friends, one with extended family, and one with the neighbors. We often looked after one another's children after school or on weekends, which frequently ended with impromptu meals together. When our younger son, Michael, was born with colic and cried for three months straight, neighbors out for their evening walks dropped in, took Michael out of our arms to hold and cuddle him, and sent us on our way, saying, "I think you need a walk more than we do."

We often joked that none of us had a life, meaning we had nothing better to do than hang out with one another, but, in fact, that was our life, and it was a good one. We made time for one another. We knew we had created something special together—we still know that. Marlene and I and our boys felt that we mattered to these neighbors; we were cared for, and we returned the caring.

Neighborliness Lost and Found

After completing her PhD program, Marlene accepted a job as a professor at the University of Waterloo and quickly was given tenure. Her normally half-hour commute from Cambridge to the campus took an hour because of traffic jams during rush hour, which kept getting worse. Michael was in the first grade, and Lucas was just entering the sixth. With me on the road so much as I started the Tamarack Institute, we considered a move back to Waterloo, to be closer not only to Marlene's job but also to our sons' schools.

We struggled with this decision for a long time. We knew it made sense to be closer to the children's schools in case something happened when we were at work. Marlene's mother lived in Waterloo and was available to help out when needed. We also knew that as she aged, she would need us more. Finally, the tough decision was made: we would buy a house near the university, leaving the neighbors who had become like family to us.

But where to move? We thought that if we could find a short street like the one we lived on in Cambridge, we would have a better chance of getting to know our neighbors and re-creating the sorts of connections we had there. We bought another fixer-upper at the end of a street with eight houses on it, and this time we allowed two months for renovations before moving in. Not one person came over to say hello during that time. We wondered if anyone else lived on the street.

School started for the children, and still no connections were made. By October, I was getting desperate. Our old neighbors, as they came to be known, had already come all the way to Waterloo to throw us a housewarming party, and yet we still had not met even one of our new neighbors. The children, feeling displaced, started making up stories about some of the neighbors and their houses, trying to scare one another about what took place in them. They were both upset that we had moved; this was their way to annoy us.

Several of our neighbors were Muslim, and I was deeply concerned that our sons would stereotype them because of their dress and other cultural differences. The bottom line was that I did not want my children to fear their neighbors. I wanted them to know their neighbors and, if not like them, at least respect them.

I remember a conversation Marlene and I had then, wondering if we had made a big mistake. We had known before we moved that it was going to be hard giving up the old neighbors. However, we had assumed that we would be connected to our new neighborhood in no time. How hard could it be to get to know your neighbors?

When only two children showed up at our front door for Halloween, I decided to take matters into my own hands. I'm not sure if it was the sugar high I was experiencing from eating all the candy we didn't give out or if it was just sheer determination, but over the next week I went door-to-door to everyone on our street and invited them to our place for a wine-and-cheese party. This was an exercise in intentional neighborliness. I was committed to finding a time when everyone could be part of it. It took me four or five rounds—telling people, "Well, Bob cannot make it that day," or "Klaus is away that weekend," or "Mary is visiting family"—until I finally got a day when everyone was available.

The day of the party arrived, and so did the people. We greeted them, and our children carried cheese and desserts to them. It seemed a bit odd that people were friendly but shy—as though they were seeing one another for the first time. Nearly an hour passed, and the only person still not there was Shirley, who, according to her husband, Bob, was working late.

Not long after, the doorbell rang, and I greeted Shirley. As I was hanging up her coat, she turned to Klaus, who was sitting by the door, extended her hand, and said, "Hi, my name is Shirley." My mouth dropped open. Such a greeting is reserved for strangers, but I knew from my walking back and forth between houses for this party that Shirley had lived on this street for fourteen years and Klaus for twelve. They lived only three houses away from each other.

That day I knew that if I was going to get to know my neighbors, it would be a long journey and require hard work. Luckily, I was a community developer by profession, but this was going to take every skill I had.

Over the next five years, things got better. Even though I had my own full-time work, traveling every other week, I organized spring and fall gatherings every year, always planning them around the dates for Ramadan to ensure that our Muslim neighbors would be able to come. I learned who had country cottages and when they were away to them. I tried to keep up with what was happening in my neighbors' lives, especially those who traveled, so that whenever I planned a get-together, I could work around their schedules, too.

In the fifth year, when Ramadan fell very late in the fall and I had several trips for work, I had to postpone the fall party to early December. Given the cold, we had to have the party in our house rather than on the street. Everyone came—even Klaus, who was undergoing chemotherapy the next day. We had a wonderful time. Marlene commented as we were cleaning up that she had wondered if our neighbors were ever going home; the party went until after eleven, with everyone staying to the end.

Later that night, the first massive snowstorm of the season hit. When I awoke in the morning, our street was snowed in, with the end of our road blocked by a pile left from the snowplow. It usually took a day or two for a smaller plow to come and open the street back up. By ten, the two Bobs who live on our street were out with their snowblowers. Soon the rest of the neighbors joined in, some with shovels, others sending goodwill to those who toiled, all of us laughing and enjoying one another and the first snow. Klaus had a chemo treatment to get to, and we were determined to get him there. In no time the street was cleared. There was pure joy in knowing one another and working together.

That evening I received this e-mail:

To Glenburn Avenue neighbors
From Vy Dyck
Subject: YOU GUYS ARE WONDERFUL

As I peered from a bedroom window I witnessed two snow-men plowing as they mutually walked up and down the road passing each other. I thought I was dreaming but when I went outside our road was clear. NOW THAT IS TEAMMANSHIP AND THE TRUE SENSE OF GIVING. WOW you guys are GREAT.

MERRY CHRISTMAS TO ALL OF YOU

P.S. I was out walking with some friends last night and they were both jealous that we had a neighborhood that not only knew who each other was but did things for each other and had get-togethers with each other. They just couldn't believe that two men from the neighborhood actually took the time to plow the entire street. :^)

Marlene and I had not created another Pheasant Avenue, but we had come closer to that reality. Now that the process has started, only good can come from it. Bob often helps clear our driveway of snow, and the other Bob is always helping Zlada with hers. Ali brings us organic eggs, and we have worked with him and Soheli to convert our broken-down basketball court into a beautiful community play area for the children on the street. Marlene, our sons, and I have converted a messy green space at the end of our street into a much prettier garden for all to enjoy.

A developer recently bought up a corner lot and wanted to significantly intensify it without neighborhood input. Because we had built trust on our street, we were able to make our collective voice heard. We overturned his plans. As I write this, we are planning a gathering for this weekend—again with 100 percent attendance expected.

The Importance of Knowing Our Neighbors

In chaotic times, knowing our neighbors is not optional. More than ever, we will want to trust our neighbors and rely on them for help, comfort, and safety.

What does it mean to be a neighbor or to live in a neighborhood? The simple act of knowing your neighbor is substantial today, but getting to know our neighbors is not really that hard, and the benefits are numerous:

- We feel safer and, more important, our children feel safer, mainly because we know something about our neighbors and their values and needs. They become real people rather than "those people."

- We can help one another. Getting Klaus to chemo was important. Knowing that if we ever needed to get to chemo, our neighbors would do the same for us—priceless.

- Doing things with our neighbors is fun! Spontaneous get-togethers, or just stopping in to visit and catch up, gives us instant access to human connection.

- We build *social capital*, whereby knowing one another turns into a reciprocal relationship of caring. When many people have this bond, a community creates an informal social safety net by which people look out for one another.

So many things can keep us from getting to know our neighbors:

- The way we build our houses means that most people retreat to their backyards when they are outside, instead of gardening at the front of their houses, where they can meet the people on their street, or sitting on the porch and seeing them as they stroll by. I know of a New York City resident who, by city law, is not allowed to garden in his front yard, and he sees the struggle between southern, front-yard cultures where neighbors meet and share gardening lore and techniques and northern, backyard cultures that keep their gardens to themselves. Better (or worse) yet for those in backyard cultures, automatic garage door openers allow neighbors to drive into their homes and not emerge in public again until, with a clanking and a whir, the door opens the next morning and they roar off to another place.

In cases like these, what are the chances of even noticing people coming and going?

- Life is just so busy. When we work away from home, we often leave early and come home late. Children go to school and then have a myriad of sports activities or lessons that take their time.

- We watch a lot of TV and surf the Internet, so we go "out" a lot less, creating fewer chances to see our neighbors.

- Many of our neighborhoods have sidewalks and bike paths that make us less reliant on cars, yet most of these walkways lead us out of the neighborhood. Neighborhoods that are purely residential lack restaurants or stores or yoga studios where we can bump into our neighbors.

- We have many different interests and come from many walks of life, causing us to assume that we have little in common. In reality, it is our differences that make us interesting.

- We belong to fewer churches, clubs, and recreational groups; therefore, even if we still meet many people, we do not do things together with them on a regular basis.

- As family members live farther away from one another, we have come to rely on professional systems of care rather than on one another to help us in times of need.

How to Get to Know Your Neighbors

There are some very concrete ways by which you can strengthen neighborliness.

- Take the initiative. If everyone waits for someone else to organize a gathering, no one will.

- Take a risk. Trust me, 80 percent of your neighbors want to know one another; all it takes is to organize an event well (see the next point), and most will come.

- Rather than just giving out a date and time and expecting people to show up, check in with them to see when might be good for them to gather (we call this "community engagement"). Take the time to entertain on dates that everyone, or at least a core group, can commit to. Not only is this efficient, in that it maximizes attendance, but also it sends the message that everyone is important and welcome. At first, you may need to go door-to-door. Embrace this, because it will help you meet people face-to-face, which is the very best organizing approach. Once you get going, you can gather everyone's e-mail and other contact information to make things much easier.

- Consider changing your front yard. We took out our entire lawn and moved our garden to the front. We also removed the railing around the porch so that we can sit and enjoy the fullness of our flowers, shrubs, fruits, and vegetables—and greet the neighbors as they pass by.

- Get out and play. Children can bring a neighborhood together, and dogs are also great at building relationships. Stop and talk while you walk.

- Consider forming a neighborhood or apartment association. This can facilitate the organization of community events, socials, and programs that will support neighborhood cohesiveness.

In this chapter, I have stressed the value and ease (though it can take work at first) of being an intentional neighbor. All other forms of community building are more difficult, and in many ways less valuable, than knowing your neighbors. By the same token, knowing your neighbors facilitates all other community-building efforts.

Social Capital

Enjoying one another, explored in the previous chapter, is deeply connected to taking care of one another. This may be seen in the work of Robert Putnam, a sociologist from Harvard University. Putnam has written extensively about the value of social interaction, which he has named *social capital*: the investment that individuals make in their communities by belonging to social clubs or civic organizations.

In researching the quality of public services in Italy, Putnam stumbled across a finding that communities with the strongest social interaction through clubs, music groups, cooperatives, unions, and the like also had the most social harmony. When he looked at communities in the United States and Canada, he discovered a correlation between the decline in clubs and civic organizations and a decline in the quality of life. He advocated that just as communities rely on financial capital (the money that makes things happen), to be successful they also need social capital.

Putnam's research has opened many people's eyes to the importance of knowing others and doing things together consistently over time—in other words, enjoying one another (as discussed in more detail in the previous chapter) and building a bond of trust as a form of organizing. This, many have come to believe, creates networks of people who learn to work together and care for one another. In his best-known book, *Bowling Alone: The Collapse and Revival of American Community*, he tells the story of a man who bowled for many years in the same league with the same people.

This relationship led to identifying a donor for a kidney that this man needed to live. Their only connection was the reciprocity they had earned over fifteen years at the bowling alley.

KATHY'S STORY   *A Quiet Force for Good*

Anita Fiegueth, a friend and part-time researcher at the Tamarack Institute for several years, shared Kathy's story with me—a dramatic example of community caring.

Anita said that when she was a teenager, her mother visited Kathy, who had multiple sclerosis and was living in a hospital. Anita's mother and Kathy had both studied nursing at the same hospital in Winnipeg. Both were married and had a son and daughter around the same age. But Anita's mother could play soccer with her kids, while Kathy was unable to move anything except her head.

One of Kathy's frustrations about needing to live in the hospital was never getting to eat her supper while it was hot, since patients had to wait for the nurses on the ward to feed them. So Anita and her mother visited every Tuesday afternoon to give Kathy her supper.

Kathy was a quiet force and a powerful example of how to live with dignity in the face of adversity. She was a good listener and a thoughtful speaker. Many people came to her to ask her advice about navigating the complexities of the hospital bureaucracy. Over the years, she had many roommates, and some of their family and friends continued to visit her even after their loved one had died or been moved to a nursing home.

One day Kathy announced that she was going to start mouth painting. With the help of an artist, she (with no artistic background) slowly started painting. Her idea was to make a painting that could be used on a Christmas card and sold as a fundraiser for the Multiple Sclerosis Society. Every year, Kathy painted a card. Her work fueled one of the society's most successful fundraising efforts.

Years later, Anita brought her own children to visit Kathy. Soon after, Kathy contracted pneumonia and decided to decline medical treatment. She had lived with MS for more than forty years and was ready to stop struggling. She had already beaten the odds: she had seen her children grow and marry, had four wonderful grandchildren, was a successful painter, and had helped innumerable people when their lives intersected with hers in the hospital.

The church was packed for Kathy's funeral, which was an inspiring tribute to a person who, with all her difficulties and physical limitations, had touched many people and created a community out of her adversity. Some might say "how sad" when they hear about Kathy's illness, but her suffering connected her to many people and brought both them and her great joy.

Caring for one another has a way of doing that.

JOSHUA'S STORY
Letting Neighborliness Take Its Course

Joshua was born without a functioning brain. For his parents, the moment of receiving this devastating news about their first child was almost more than they could bear. The doctors gave them a choice: keep their son on a version of life support for his entire life or "let nature take its course."

Joshua's parents brought their anguish and dilemma to their church, whose members formed a deep circle of support around this young couple. They met weekly to sit in silence and pray. Every day a meal was dropped off at the home and a doctor in the congregation visited.

When Joshua died a month later, more than three hundred people came to his funeral. Stories of life and death were shared and many tears were shed in a collective grieving of a life that had lasted only a month. Many said that it was the most meaningful funeral they had ever attended, a moment of shared humanity and vulnerability.

Joshua had orchestrated a symphony of caring and changed a community forever.

MILDRED'S STORY *Enriching Relationships*

Mildred is a developmentally challenged adult who lives a life of joy in a L'Arche community. L'Arche was founded in 1964 by Jean Vanier, son of Canadian Governor General Georges Vanier and Pauline Vanier, when he opened his home to two men with disabilities in the French town of Trosly-Breuil. L'Arche has grown into an international organization operating on every continent in forty countries.

At L'Arche, Mildred is part of a small, faith-based community of friendship between people who have disabilities and their caregivers, often young people with a goal of developing a lifelong support system. They highlight the unique capacity of persons with disabilities like Mildred to enrich relationships and to build a community where the values of compassion, inclusion, and diversity are embraced and lived by each person.

Mildred feels acceptance and joy living in community with caregivers who have committed to living in community with her.

She experiences and contributes to the fullness of community and lives a life of purpose.

Survival of the Kindest

The stories of Kathy, Joshua, and Mildred highlight the conclusion of University of California psychology professor Dacher Keltner in *Born to Be Good: The Science of a Meaningful Life*, that "the emotions that promote the meaningful life are organized according to an interest in the welfare of others. Compassion shifts the mind in ways that increase the likelihood of taking pleasure in the improved welfare of others." In other words, we are hardwired to care for one another. Keltner goes on to discuss this as a mutual sort of relationship. We instinctively know that if we benefit the lives of others, they, in turn, will benefit our lives. Working for the good of all increases the benefit for each of us.

Charles Darwin is known for his "survival of the fittest" theory. The common description is that the most able animals will continue to evolve, while weaker species will be eliminated over time. This interpretation often has been used to justify what some call a "dog eat dog" world. The biggest dog, the most aggressive dog, will always get what it wants, and the others will get what is left over. This has so deeply entered the ethos of our culture that we have adopted competition as the core value by which we live and the GDP as the chief measure of our success.

What is most often overlooked is Darwin's work in his later years, as he observed not only competition but also cooperation in animals. As Jeremy Rifkin observes in his book *The Empathic Civilization: The Race to Global Consciousness in a World in Crisis*, "Darwin came to believe that survival of the fittest is as much about cooperation, symbiosis, and reciprocity as it is about individual competition and that the most fit are just as likely to enter in cooperative bonds with their fellows." Taking care of one another and looking out for one another has been an evolutionary prerequisite. It is why we have survived.

We are naturally an empathic people, says Rifkin, a world-renowned economist and writer. We naturally care. As young as two years of age, children actively try to alleviate the suffering of a crying child by bringing over a toy, giving a hug, or taking that child to his or her mother. Empathy, according to Rifkin, is the act of entering into the emotional state of someone else's suffering and absorbing it as if it were one's own pain.

"We are not just a species whose fundamental reason for being is survival," writes Rifkin. "We are by nature an affectionate species that continuously seeks to broaden and deepen our relationship and connections to others, in effect to transcend ourselves by participating in more expansive communities of meaning." As a result, "our increasingly complex social structures provide the vehicles for the journey." Yes! Community is our natural way of being, and caring is at the center of community.

When we believe that we need to be the fastest, the smartest, and the best, we create walls around ourselves that separate us from others. When we believe that by cooperating, caring, and reaching out to others, we will harness the wisdom within our diversity, we create the conditions for community. It is our choice how we want to live and what consequences will result.

A theory known as "survival of the kindest" is growing in popularity. It states that evolution is more a cooperative process than a competitive one. Species that have been able to collaborate and learn from one another are much more adaptable to their environments and able to respond to the changing circumstances in which they find themselves. Survival of the fittest was not just about being stronger, better, and faster. Individual animals did not survive, but species ultimately evolved. The more the members of a species worked together, learned from one another, and cared for one another, the more likely they were to survive.

Caring for one another and working together are at the heart of community. It is how we build a sense of belonging. When we create an ethos of caring, kind individuals not only fare better but also are able to evoke kindness in others, thus prompting co-operative exchange.

In conclusion, while it is not a simple point-A-to-point-B process, place and proximity matter: community is built from the neighborhood out, from knowing your neighbor to sharing your life with your neighbor to caring for one another in your neighborhood to building social capital by forming associations, clubs, faith communities, and so on. In the previous chapter we looked at the power of joy in community; in this chapter we have looked at the power of neighborliness, caring, and empathy. Now it is time to see how all of this gathers momentum to help communities make a difference, together, for a better world.

8 Working Together for a Better World

Kindle in us love's compassion so that everyone may see
In our fellowship the promise of a new humanity.
—FROM THE HYMN "HEART WITH
LOVING HEARTS UNITED"

I RECENTLY ATTENDED a play at my sister's church. She not only acted in the play but also had assisted in producing it. The proceeds went to support several Muslim refugee families that the church was helping to come settle in Canada. Mennonite churches had joined together all over the region to bring an entire extended family from a refugee camp to settle in Waterloo Region. I was impressed by this act because it was a collective act of caring with no interest or intention for benefit or gain by the churches.

The lunch we enjoyed before the play was provided by the local Muslim community. About fifty Palestinian Canadians had come to see the play and lend their support to this traditional Mennonite church's cause. It was their way of saying thank-you. I cannot tell you the joy I felt as I ate amazing Middle Eastern food and watched Muslim and Mennonite mothers and grandmothers working side by side. Fathers set tables and chased after children who, though worlds apart, were mingling as if they had been friends for years.

I'm not sure what impressed me more, traditional Muslim families coming to a Christian church to join in a common cause or Mennonite mothers opening a kitchen used most often for cooking potatoes and turkey to make traditional rice, chicken skewers, hummus, and tabbouleh salad.

The play was meant to juxtapose meaningful stories of people who had just returned from a volunteer assignment trying to help resolve conflicts in Israel with humorous stories of people engaged in small but everyday conflicts at home. It was a wonderful play, showing the complexity of conflict and how difficult as well as simple bringing peace to a situation can be. The play concluded with one simple conclusion: selfless giving is at the root of peace.

In these chaotic times, we need more than ever to be working for a better world. This is not to say that there is no good in the world right now. There is a lot of good, and much hope too. But just as a human body breaks down when it is overworked and not cared for, so the earth is ill because of its residents' unsustainable practices. Environmentally and economically, a sickness has set in, and together we must change the conditions that have caused this illness. In some cases, this change is something that we can help others to agree on doing together, such as limiting the use of fossil fuels or consuming food and buying items that are produced locally. But in most cases, the change must start with us and our communities.

Working for a better world is not only good for the earth; it is also good for us. Some call it "mutual aid" and others "enlightened self-interest." Volunteers often say that when they serve, they receive far more than they give.

When we work together for a better world, we receive many benefits, including the power of collective altruism and the joy of giving and receiving.

The Power of Collective Altruism

A single tsunami ravages many communities around the world. Amid the horrible aftermath, another sort of tsunami arises as the world unites, giving millions of dollars and tireless support to help those who are suffering. As described in chapter 7, young people absorbed in their very involved lives get up early on a Saturday morning simply because they are asked, and unite to deliver ten thousand pies from a truck to the arena where they will be sold in one of many events that will contribute to raising more than $300,000 that day for world relief. Their work not only looks effortless, but it radiates energy and joy, and all who experience this marvelous scene are rejuvenated.

This is the power of collective altruism. Like a prism concentrating light, when we merge individual altruism and collective purpose/intention/determination/resolve, we create the conditions for an exponential effect for good. This effect often seems to create an energy that fuels the collective resolve. As collective altruism helps the sufferers of a tsunami or raises funds for world relief, it opens hearts, blurring the lines between giving and receiving and forging community.

I have described the experience of belonging in community as being with others over time, prompting mutual acts of caring and the merging of individual identities with the group's identity. Those doing the work also experience the collective force and energy of the altruism and thus the connection for good. There is just something about working together for the betterment of others or the world in general. A metaphysical bond emerges between people, and in no time complete strangers feel as if they have been connected for a long time.

The Joy of Giving and Receiving

Habitat for Humanity is one of the world's best-known charities. It does wonderful work, providing housing for impoverished people around the world. When I talk to my friends and clients about this great charity, I often share the other important benefit of its work: its impact on the volunteers who participate in building the houses. When a Habitat house is built, dozens of people volunteer with the person(s) who will receive the house, pouring the foundation, erecting the walls, shingling the roof, finishing the drywall, and laying the carpets. The actual build can be done in just a few days because so many people work together so well.

I have never talked to a Habitat volunteer who hasn't said that this was a deeply meaningful experience. All feel a tremendous sense of accomplishment as they work as a team. They also describe the sense of community they experienced and speak of how they made lifelong friends after working and eating and enjoying their time together. The ability to work side by side with the family receiving the home made their giving real.

We work together for the good of others not just because it makes us feel good, as some cynics like to observe. The giving-and-receiving relationship provides a form of mutuality and takes the work beyond charity. I have called this "restoring our humanity." When we are able to express our caring with others, a collective energy has the potential to emerge that opens all of our hearts and turns giving into receiving and receiving into giving. We are able to exist together within the rawness of our shared humanity.

I think of Kate, who belongs to a local Rotary Club, which gives her a wonderful community of like-minded people. They meet each week for lunch to listen to someone who is making a difference in their community. They support young people and raise funds for community projects and for the work of Rotary International. Like many service clubs, they do a lot of good for their community.

Kate had been a member for a long time when she shared the following observations:

> Our Rotary Club has become like family to me. This happens when you share as much time together as we do. We are, though, a club dedicated to service, as reflected in our mission, which is to provide service to others, promote integrity, and advance world understanding, goodwill, and peace through its fellowship of business, professional, and community leaders.
>
> There are times, though, when we get tired and start to feel stale. It is hard to keep such a community active. Yet without fail, when we start to feel stodgy, someone will say, "It is time to do a project together." So together we design and implement something that makes our community better—maybe it is a fundraiser, helping a school, or building a playground.
>
> This work draws us out of one another and into the lives and meaning of others. We feel renewed, hopeful, and positive. Not just because we did something for others— that is for sure part of it—but because we did it together. As we opened ourselves to someone else's need, we opened ourselves to one another.

And then there's Nina, who believed deeply in the importance of connecting her friends and neighbors to local farms and the food they produced. First she went to the many farmers she knew and asked if they would sell her fresh and organic produce on a weekly basis. Then she advertised this to her friends.

Every Friday morning, Nina and her father, Wendell, drove to the farms and picked up the produce. Each Friday afternoon, more than one hundred of Nina's friends gathered at her home, armed with bags and boxes to buy the local produce.

It was a bit like a weekly party: parents brought their children to play together, and strangers became friends and often spent up to an hour longer than they needed to, visiting and enjoying one another. At times, people brought their guitars to play and others some home baking to share.

Many volunteered, as the idea caught on and grew. A community formed around the desire for fresh organic produce and the joy of participating in building a better world.

When we invest in community, a little bit can go a long way toward building a better world. I hope that the following examples will give you the courage to make a difference.

Nick enjoyed his neighborhood but did not feel safe in it. Seven break-ins had happened in two months, with substantial damage each time. Though the police were quick to respond, they admitted that they could not be present twenty-four hours a day. Nick decided to start a neighborhood watch program, designed to "help neighbors watch out for neighbors." By getting connected with one another, neighbors were able to recognize strangers and any suspicious activity. The program, according to the Ottawa Police Services website, "combats crime in the most effective way—before it starts." Nick and his neighbors learned to take care of one another and created a safer neighborhood.

Joe is a carpenter who enjoys his neighborhood. He wants to build a workshop where he can store his tools and machines and also complete projects needed for his business. Instead of building it on his own, Joe is hoping to involve his neighbors and make it a community workshop. He envisions a place where ideas as well as tools can be exchanged, where people can visit often and enjoy one another's company, where a helping hand will be available for those who need it. What an appropriate venue: a workshop where people build community.

Bill sold a large business at a relatively young age. You would think that with all his success and power, his beautiful family, and the capacity to buy anything his heart desired, he would just retire and be happy. But Bill wanted to invest his wealth to build a better world. When Bill was introduced to me, he got right to the point. He wanted to hear my story about how I decided to devote myself full time to building community and to learn firsthand my observations and experiences. Bill could see that joy can come to those who commit themselves to a life of service, using their money to make a difference. He and his wife, Janet, decided to fund the organizations of a dozen people whose work inspired them and to bring these twelve into a community once a year to learn and support one another. Much joy, indeed! Bill then founded an organization called Social Capital Partners and dedicated himself full time to working with young people living in poverty, providing them with the skills, work experience, and connections that would make them job ready.

More Than a Roof (MTR) nurtures joy by building homes for people moving out of poverty. This wonderful organization not only provides affordable shelter but also rebuilds the physical, mental, spiritual, and financial health of residents, and introduces or helps restore healthy peer relationships, including reconnecting with family. Candela Place is an MTR community in downtown Vancouver, British Columbia, that supports homeless single people struggling with addiction and/or mental health issues. When I visited there recently, several in that community talked about their successes:

- Jake shared at length how coming to Candela turned things around for him. He has been sober for seven years now, he said, adding that the best way to heal is to get outside yourself, which is what he believes volunteering can do—it can "help you walk in someone else's shoes for a while."

- Martha spoke next about her volunteer work in prisons and churches and on the street.

- Then came Tammy, who runs the library; Bill, who manages the community store; and Joan and Sally, who are fantastic painters.

- Gord, a poet, was next, followed by Melissa, who is writing a book.

It is amazing how productive people can be when they have a home.

Rita loves to garden. When the local homeless shelter put out a call for fresh produce, she brought an idea to her church: Could they work together to grow fresh produce for the homeless shelter? Several members of the congregation had land they were not using, and in no time a half-acre of land was prepared. After dialogue with people at the homeless shelter, they found out that beans and corn were a favorite of many. The garden was planted and the produce grown and harvested, with the extras frozen. The homeless shelter now has some of the tastiest and most nutritious beans and corn around, all year long. Rita and her church community enjoyed one another, bonded in the work, and built a deep sense of connection to one another and those in need in their community.

Joe loves to cook almost as much as he loves visiting with people and working for a better world. Joe always thought that there was need for a place where these three loves could happen together. So he started Queen Street Commons in downtown Kitchener, Ontario. His first idea was to serve affordable, locally produced vegetarian food and fair trade coffee. His second idea was to create an informal and inviting space with large tables, a stage, and even movie-projection capability, where people could gather to discuss and enjoy ideas and art. His third idea was to bring together people from many diverse walks of life. Whether they were professionals working downtown, homeless people, or new Canadians, everyone was welcomed and encouraged to volunteer and share their gifts with one another. Joe has created a space for connection. A homeless man suffering from mental illness comes in every day to play the piano, and does so beautifully. Every Thursday, immigrants wanting to learn English come to the Speak English Café and converse with volunteers. Some students come to learn and others just to study on the comfortable furniture. At lunchtime, busy professionals come to eat gourmet vegetarian food or pick up a beautiful coffee. Queen Street Commons—the name says it all.

Is Community Possible?

We have moved along in this book, exploring the four acts of community building that feed into the option of deepening community. The challenge, however, is to go from knowing that deep community is possible to joining together and making it so. It's our choice to make.

9 Making the Choice for Deep Community

To dare is to lose one's footing momentarily.
Not to dare is to lose oneself.

—SØREN KIERKEGAARD, NINETEENTH-
CENTURY DANISH PHILOSOPHER

A THEME OF THIS BOOK is that because of the complexity of our times, community is not so much chosen for us as by us. It is not a Pollyanna choice. It is a choice made in the midst of very real struggles in our own life and in our world. As chaos is visited upon us because of our environmental and economic choices, we will be called on to make many difficult decisions. These decisions will indicate our allegiances. Will we pull our borders in and be satisfied with shallow community? Will we turn against others in fear-based community? Or will we move toward others to create joy-based deep community?

As we have seen, the latter choice is a process; it is one that is worth reviewing here as we come to the close of this book.

Sharing Our Story

The journey begins as we share our stories, be they stories of fears or of joy. Sharing helps us to open up, to become vulnerable, to hear other people's stories. Thus do we begin to work together to distinguish truth from untruth and rational fear from irrational fear, to determine what we might do together. When we really hear one another, the bond of community is forged between us. We smile at each other; we feel warmth and joy as if we are home. In these times, we must make it a priority to take time for community. We need one another now, and we will need one another even more as times become more difficult.

Enjoying One Another

As we continue to share our stories, and do so with the same players over time, reciprocity and trust grow between us. This is an investment in deepening community, and the dividends this investment pays will be crucial to us in times of need. When we enjoy one another in a community we have invested in, we become a collective witness to the events around us. We can celebrate our achievements and those of our children together. How sweet are the victories and even failures that are experienced in community!

Taking Care of One Another

Reciprocity and trust have a wonderful effect: reaching out to help one another becomes as natural as breathing. We take care of one another not only because it is the right thing to do, and not only because people will help us if we help them, but primarily because the bond of love that has grown between us moves us to do so. Mutual acts of caring that happen often forge a sense of belonging. When we feel we belong, we feel safe and fulfilled, and when we feel safe and fulfilled, we can dare to develop hope and common purpose. We have the strength to overcome, together, almost any challenge that comes our way.

Building a Better World Together

The above three acts of community—sharing our stories, enjoying one another, and taking care of one another—give us energy for the fourth act of deepening community: building a better world together. In fact, we become a force for change that is unstoppable. The work of restoring our communities feels light and possible. We no longer feel alone in our fear or hopeless in our dreams; rather, we have the courage to see our dreams become real.

Dreams and Reality

As we know from the life of Martin Luther King Jr., dreams of substance have a way of becoming real. King had a dream, and his dream, of justice between the races, has come true—not fully, not without many backward steps, not without so much more ground to take, because nothing in life is perfect, but true nonetheless.

A memory from my Mennonite youth—I hope that you will allow me one more—bears on this topic of dreams, or daydreams, in my case.

I performed a task every day from the age of six to eighteen, one with an unintended consequence (unintended by my parents, who gave me the task): learning to dream. For two or more hours a day, I collected eggs from the nearly twelve thousand chickens on our farm—I was assigned to gather 350 dozen eggs—walking down aisles of cages behind an egg wagon that was six feet long and about three feet high, as it lumbered along on its large balloonlike tires.

As I threw my arms back and forth with the rhythm of a fly fisherman, picking up three eggs in each hand and laying them into cartons, my mind could be otherwise occupied. I learned to daydream in extreme detail. Not only did I come up with big, bold ideas, but also I used the time to break them into the micro details and processes that would see them come to reality (if only in my mind).

I grew up wanting to make a difference in the world, so this skill of mentally turning dreams into reality has proven to be useful. I have been extremely lucky both in my dreaming and in finding so many colleagues and friends (my deep community) with whom to dream the same dreams together. Over a period of thirty years, the art of dreaming in detail has allowed us to start and/or build a dozen organizations, raise an estimated $100 million for charitable causes, and help more than a quarter million people live a better life.

In my work as director of Tamarack Insitute, I have been privileged to lead people nationwide in community initiatives to reduce poverty and increase the riches of intentional neighborliness.

For me, large-scale initiatives to bring together the poor, existing community organizations, the efforts of governments at all levels, and private and public businesses begin with dreams. Dreaming is my way of considering every possible angle and all the scenarios of a situation well before it becomes a reality. For me, a dream is much more than a wish; it is a full-color, multidimensional window into the future.

For example, more than twenty years ago, I was privileged to lead an organization that provided reconciliation experiences through job training for young people living amid "the Troubles" in Northern Ireland. Several times a year, twenty young people—ten Catholic and ten Protestant—arrived in Cambridge, Ontario, and were billeted for three months in the homes of people, many of whom had come from Northern Ireland or the Republic of Ireland.

The program was based on the need to break the cycle of fear and hatred between Protestants and Catholics and, in turn, stop the violence. Many of the Catholic young people with whom we were working had never had a Protestant friend and had never been in the home of a Protestant, and vice versa. Our work was to challenge the stereotypes and, over a three-month period, build a new story in the hearts and minds of these young people.

Many of them were from lower-income communities and, given the state of the economy in their country, had found it difficult to find jobs. They were vulnerable to the violence in their communities, for the prospect of a bleak future, economically, made them fertile ground for terrorist recruiters.

We saw job training as a way to recruit them into the reconciliation-training program we were offering. Once these young people lived, worked, and partied together away from the norms and patterns of their native neighborhoods, we were able—they were able—to change their attitudes and beliefs forever.

We learned that fear and hate, when challenged appropriately, can be changed, particularly when there is hope for a better future. The program was part of a much larger peace effort that has since stopped the killing in Northern Ireland.

It is because of dreams—not just mine, but those of many fellow workers in this great task of deepening community—that many thousands of people have seen their poverty reduced and have more work, better housing, healthier and safer families, and affordable transportation. It is because of dreams that thousands of children are happier in better day care, have more friends, and receive books on their birthdays and presents at Christmas. It is because of dreams that people with developmental disabilities have more community and meaning in their lives. And it is because of dreams that whole communities have learned to change their circumstances, reduce poverty and crime, and improve their neighborhoods and conditions for generations to come.

The needs of our families, neighborhoods, and countries are still great—and, in these chaotic times, will become all the more so. But we know what we must do as a community. We must keep dreaming and sharing our dreams and hopes with one another. And we must keep making these dreams come true by acting on them as a community but never against another community. Acting in this way will be challenging but will be done with a lightness of being if we look out for and include one another. It is in the work of restoring our neighborhoods, cities, and beyond that we will see the result of dreams that are dreamed in deep community.

And what is deep community? It is the process of finding joy—much joy!—together.

Five Hundred Voices

A LL OF MY WRITING—especially *Deepening Community*—
arises from my curiosity about the ethos of community.
What are people thinking about community? How would they
describe their experience? As I began my plans for writing this
book, I wanted to invite many people to join me in my inquiry.

Together with Tamarack staff, I decided that the most active
two thousand members of Tamarack's learning community, which
had at that time grown to about eight thousand people, would be
a perfect group to ask about their experience of community. These
are people who are well informed and think about community
daily, most of them as professionals, people with the ability to
harvest deep insights and wisdom from their efforts to make
their cities and neighborhoods better places to live. More than
five hundred of these individuals responded—a remarkable 25
percent response rate!

I wanted to know if they really cared about the place of community in their personal lives and how they thought about it. Our
goal was to gather much information and then boil it down to
more easily understood ideas. At Tamarack, we sometimes refer
to this as "maple syruping" ideas. See www.deepeningcommunity
.com for an explanation of and complete results of the survey.

Designing the Survey

The topic of community is broad and complex. I wanted not to create and run a scientific experiment but to put together a survey that would reflect the questions I personally had about community. I wanted people to share their feelings about their sense of community, their personal definitions, and their ideas. I wanted to evoke their inner wisdom. I also wanted to be able to report these results back to them and make their ideas public—to gather their collective wisdom into one place and give it living form.

We decided to use a survey technique called a Common Meaning Questionnaire, which is described in more detail in my book *Community Conversations*. This method is loosely based on Eidetics, a process founded by systems researcher Henry Evering that relies on Socratic principles. Using questions that build on one another, it assumes that every individual possesses innate knowledge, a unique way of seeing things, and the ability to find solutions by cooperating with others for mutual benefit. The questions help people express their meaning and their perception of words and concepts.

The researchers then deconstructed the building blocks of statements in participants' answers and examined multiple-meaning statements for the larger concepts we were exploring. This is a unique approach that allows us to explore words and concepts that people hold in common. We had participants write down the meaning behind the words, which caused themes of common understanding to emerge from the data. We were then able to quantify the number of times participants expressed a certain feeling or concept. The following is a sampling of the questions that were addressed:

- What does "community" mean to you?
- What does "the benefit of community" mean to you?
- What does "belonging to community" mean to you?
- What does "identity in community" mean to you?
- When do you most profoundly experience community?
- What builds community for you?
- What causes community to break down for you?
- What do people do when they experience fear as a community?
- When do you most feel a sense of community?

For the full survey analysis, go to www.deepeningcommunity.com.

With Thanks

*t*O WRITE a book about community truly takes a community. First, because without him you would not be reading this book, I must thank Donald G. Bastian, a gifted editor of more than a thousand books. He has given his life to the art of making books and is a magnificent artist. Donald captures a manuscript in his mind while reading, as if he has a photographic memory; takes it apart; and rebuilds it, as though it were a jigsaw puzzle, into a book that people can actually understand. As I have shared with Donald many times, I am not a writer but rather an activist who needs to write. For all those activists who have a story bursting inside them, I wish you a Donald.

I want to thank Steve Piersanti of Berrett-Koehler Publishers, who worked with Donald and me for eighteen months through six drafts of the manuscript. As every author I have spoken to who has published with Berrett-Koehler has shared with me, to work with Steve is a true gift, as is working with his amazing team. This is no ordinary publishing company.

Peter Block is a mentor and a friend and the one who introduced me to Steve and the team at Berrett-Koehler, wrote the foreword to this book, and lifted my heart throughout the writing.

Will Winterfeld traveled with me to Memphis, Tennessee; Athens, Georgia (as well as to Comer and Atlanta in that state, to observe an organization called Jubilee Partners); Washington,

D.C.; Cape Croker, Ontario; and beyond to visit communities in research for this book. His search for community, his life living in community, his family, his friendship and wisdom—all influenced the journey of this book, and for that I consider him a coauthor. He always made this project seem urgent; his energy sustained me throughout.

My family inspires and for some joyful reason always supports me. Michael, Lucas, and Marlene—thank you for walking with me for more than five years of writing and a lifetime of seeking community together. Special recognition goes to Michael and his friends for writing and producing an amazing rap song and video about the book. Many thanks to my brother Henry for opening his home to me when I most needed it, creating a writer's retreat with great food, wine, and walks, and to my sisters, Rita and Lorraine, for always caring for me and my brother Frank. Thanks to Erwin and Connie Braun (a fellow writer) for the many hours spent discussing family and our history. Thanks to the Walls, my many cousins, aunts, and uncles (especially Uncle Pete, who hosted many a family gathering), who together raised me; I owe all of you much gratitude for living community, creating mutual acts of caring—often—and making me feel that I belonged.

There are others I am so grateful to: my team and board at the Tamarack Institute for Community Engagement, for your dedication and patience; Anita Fieguth, who spent endless hours reviewing and sorting the five hundred surveys that informed this book; and Joyce Hollyday, who edited the first draft of the manuscript. And finally, what a lovely, collaborative approach publishing can be in these marvelous times. My thanks to the many who commented on early drafts of the book, the nearly seven hundred people who voted on a cover design, plus the 633 who helped choose the title.

There was a time when writing this book came to a standstill. Something called me to GilChrist, a retreat center owned by the Fetzer Institute near Three Hills, Michigan. While there, I had a special awakening and revelation that took the book in a new direction. Those seven days changed me forever. I wrote this poem to mark this time.

GILCHRIST

Awake, awakening like
the cold releasing from
the morning dew

The quiet is creeping in
filling my restlessness with
the knowing rooted deep within

Today your embrace is strong
I open to the song
held for centuries in your skin.

Sources Cited

Block, Peter. *Community: The Structure of Belonging.* San Francisco: Berrett-Koehler Publishers, 2008.

Bohm, David. *Wholeness and the Implicate Order.* London and New York: Routledge, 1980.

Briskin, Alan, Sheryl Erickson, John Ott, and Tom Callanan. *The Power of Collective Wisdom: And the Trap of Collective Folly.* San Francisco: Berrett-Koehler Publishers, 2009.

Brown, Stuart, M.D., and Christopher Vaughan. *Play: How It Shapes the Brain, Opens the Imagination, and Invigorates the Soul.* New York: Penguin, 2009.

Capra, Fritjof. *The Hidden Connections: A Science for Sustainable Living.* New York: Random House, 2002.

Durkheim, Emile. *Suicide: A Study in Sociology.* Robin Buss, transl. New York: Penguin Books, 2006 (1897).

Epp, Marlene. *Women Without Men: Mennonite Refugees of the Second World War.* Toronto: University of Toronto Press, 2000.

Horney, Karen. *Our Inner Conflicts: A Constructive Theory of Neurosis.* New York: W. W. Norton, reissue edition, 1992.

Keltner, Dacher. *Born to Be Good: The Science of a Meaningful Life.* New York: W. W. Norton, 2009.

Lasch, Christopher. *The Minimal Self: Psychic Survival in Troubled Times*. New York: W. W. Norton, 1985.

Ornish, Dean. *Love and Survival: The Scientific Basis for the Healing Power of Intimacy*. New York: HarperCollins, 1998.

Ott, John. See Briskin, Alan.

Putnam, Robert D. *Bowling Alone: The Collapse and Revival of American Community*. New York: Simon & Schuster, 2000.

Putnam, Robert D., and Lewis M. Feldstein. *Better Together: Restoring the American Community*. New York: Simon & Schuster, 2004.

Riera, José, Senior Policy Adviser, Policy Development and Evaluation, UNHCR (United Nations High Commissioner for Refugees). "Climate change, migration, and human displacement: Presentation to the Second Conference on adaptation to climate change in developing countries," *The Hague*, November 25, 2008. http://www.unhcr.org/492eb4e02.pdf.

Rifkin, Jeremy. *The Empathic Civilization: The Race to Global Consciousness in a World in Crisis*. New York: Tarcher/Penguin, 2009.

Tutu, Desmond. *No Future Without Forgiveness*. New York: Image, 2000.

Walls, Jeannette. *The Glass Castle: A Memoir*. New York: Simon & Schuster, 2005.

Wheatley, Margaret J. *Finding Our Way: Leadership for an Uncertain Future*. San Francisco: Berrett-Koehler Publishers, 2005.

Index

About Paul Born

*W*HEN FOUNDING THE charity
Tamarack Institute for Community Engagement in 2001 with
philanthropist and business leader
Alan Broadbent, Paul Born titled his
first speech "Seeking the Possibilities
of Community." The title surprised
even him, because he had been called
on that day to talk about the technical
process of change in cities and how

community engagement and collaboration can lead to a larger
collective impact. Even in those early days of the institute's research—long before its work transformed how social issues like
poverty were being addressed across the country, changing more
than fifty government policies, supporting over two hundred social
innovations, and reducing poverty for more than two hundred
thousand people—Paul and his team understood that there was
a direct correlation between people's sense of community and
their willingness to improve the conditions of those who lived
around them.

In 1998, as Paul, who then directed the Community Opportunities Development Association (CODA), and his team were
honored by the United Nations Human Settlements Programme

as one of the forty Habitat best practices in the world, Nicholas You, who had flown in from Nairobi, Kenya, to present the award, stated, "We give you this award not only because you have reduced poverty for thousands of people, but more importantly because through your work you have created what will become known as a human problem solving machine [technique]." A technique that senior leaders at DuPont Canada and partners in Tamarack's work later would call "community potentialization."

Paul has always been fascinated by community. He grew up the son of refugees in a deep community of about one hundred families, all of whom had suffered the plight of mass starvation and had fled murder, rape, and oppression. As in many of the families in his community, both of his grandfathers had been executed at the hands of Stalin. Paul lived in fear as part of a people who came to Canada to heal, to start anew.

It is these experiences that drove Paul to write *Deepening Community*. In part, the process of deepening community is his journey to understand the possibilities of community in these chaotic times; it is also to explore how we might experience joy together in a world that seems to be unraveling. In all of his writing, speaking, and community work, Paul makes the case that living in joy together can help us transform our neighborhoods, our cities, our countries, and ultimately our world.

Paul is the author of four books, including the national bestseller *Community Conversations*, and founder of three national organizations. He is internationally recognized for his innovative approaches to community development. In 2013, Paul was elected to be a senior Ashoka Fellow, part of the world's largest network of social innovators: "This Senior Fellowship distinction recognizes Paul's significant contribution as an influencer and thought leader in the economic development sector."

As cofounder and president of the Tamarack Institute, Paul has spent the past twelve years with his team building a think tank and lab to grow professional capacity in the areas of collaborative leadership, community engagement, collective impact, and place-based innovation. More than fourteen thousand members from all around the world participate in Tamarack's learning communities and generate over five million page views on the Tamarack website (www.tamarackcommunity.ca) annually as they learn together. Paul is an activist and motivational speaker who travels in the United States, in Canada, and around the globe sharing his message of how we can deepen community, work collaboratively to achieve a collective impact, and, in the process, change the circumstances of those in need.

Connect with Paul at www.paulborn.ca.

Join the Deepening Community Campaign

www.deepeningcommunity.org

A Conversation to Shape Our Future

I AM PRETTY SURE that as a reader of this book, you would have no issue with the statement "Whatever the problem, community is the answer." For those of us who are intentional about community, it is hard to imagine how there might ever be another solution besides involving those we care about to share our concerns and needs and to work together to make things right.

Let's Talk

I believe that people want to talk about the future of community in their lives and the growing need for community in these chaotic times. An increasing number of people want to be able to rely on their neighbors and families and feel the assurance that when times are tough, they can reach out to others.

I do believe that this need for a good heart-to-heart between us is about more than just fear. There is an awareness rising within humanity: a growing belief that relationships trump things and that if we are going to build a better world, getting connected, enjoying one another, and working together to build our future is the solution. Yes, a growing belief that community is the answer.

Deepening Community

To facilitate these conversations, the Tamarack Institute (www
.tamarackcommunity.org) has launched a campaign to help people to talk and, in turn, learn together about the possibilities of
community. The campaign is called Deepening Community, and
it is based on explorations of community in his book of the same
name.

In order to create spaces for and inspire conversation, Tamarack is launching the following initiatives:

ONE THOUSAND CONVERSATIONS

We want to inspire one thousand conversations about community
by 2015 and have these recorded at www.deepeningcommunity.org.
We plan to group themes that arise from these conversations and
produce learning guides and policy statements to strengthen community and investments in community. Ultimately, we want to
explore the statement "Whatever the problem, community is the
answer." To support this campaign, please host a conversation and
then join the learning community at www.deepeningcommunity
.org to post what you learned together.

DEEPENINGCOMMUNITY.ORG

This website is a learning community where you can share your
stories and engage with other community seekers. On this site,
you can build your profile, blog, engage in groups, and attend
online events and small-group conversations. You will find an
amazing library of resources and papers to fuel your curiosity
and build your knowledge about community. Once you join this
learning community, you will receive a free e-magazine, which
connects members on a monthly basis. This learning community

is open to anyone and is led by a group of ten thought leaders and a community animator.

BOOK CLUBS AND MORE

We have produced many free materials in connection with publication of *Deepening Community*, including a Learning Guide that can be downloaded at www.deepeningcommunity.org and used by people to become inspired and learn together about community and how to deepen the experience of community. At this site, you will find the following:

- A book club guide
- A special offer for groups of twenty or more learning together
- The story behind the book, sharing my writing journey and a deep revelation I received at GilChrist
- The survey results of more than five hundred people who helped shape this book
- Stories from other community seekers
- Exercises to support your exploration
- A guide to host your own community conversations
- And more

NEIGHBORS

There is growing interest in neighbors. Communities all around the world are hosting neighbor days, encouraging people to get out and meet one another. We want to help fuel this movement, so we have started to sponsor approaches that deepen community in our own neighborhood. As all this work is unfolding, we are starting a larger conversation to discuss how policy can be written and adopted at a city level to support neighborhood solutions to local issues and the kinds of programs that neighborhoods might use to deepen community.

Please join us at www.deepeningcommunity.org.

Reading Circles

tHE LEARNING COMMUNITIES at Tamarack love to be in conversation with one another. It is no wonder that *Community Conversations*, the previous book by Tamarack's founder and president, Paul Born, became a Canadian bestseller. Born's most recent book, *Deepening Community*, is the perfect platform for conversations, whether with a group of friends, workmates, a faith community, or neighbors. Read this book with others and then come together for some great conversations. Here are some topics and questions for discussion. Also remember to go to www .deepeningcommunity.com for more guides, exercises, and stories to make your journey toward a deeper community easier and more effective.

Community in Chaotic Times

What is causing you to search for community? What are you finding, or failing to find? What is your first memory of community? What will your children's memory of community be? How do we overcome our fear in these chaotic times? With whom do we connect to make sense of what is going on? How do we get ready for what is coming? What is your story? What will your story be?

Living Afraid Together

When did you last seek out others who were like you because you were afraid of those who were not? What do people do when they are afraid? What happens when you are afraid? How easy is it to depersonalize someone? What happens when we create an "us and them" scenario? What does community become when we organize against others? What is the possibility of community then?

Telling Your Story

Do you want to deepen your experience of community? Where do you belong? When do you experience community in your life? What is missing? What more are you seeking? What is community? How can you make community a bigger part of your life? How can you have a better quality of community in your life? How can you increase possibilities for community? How do you know that you're where you belong? How do you deepen your experience of community?

Enjoying One Another

In what ways do you believe that community is good for you? For your children? What brings joy for you? Is this different from happiness? What memories of joy do you have from experiences of community? Do you have this joy in community now? What has changed for you? How are your communities changing? How might joy be a bigger part of your community life? What are five things you can do in community that would bring more joy to your life?

Caring for One Another

Why does it matter to find places where you belong and are cared for and can give care? Who will be there for you when you are old, to keep you from isolation and loneliness? We hear often that we should prepare for retirement by saving our money; why do we hear so infrequently about the importance of building solid relationships to build up our "community bank"? How in our busy lives do we find community? If the opportunity for community is all around us, why is it so elusive? If caring communities are so full of promise, should they not be easier to attain? If community is natural to our existence, shouldn't we just reach out more?

Working Together for a Better World

When have you seen collective altruism change something? How do people work together to have a collective impact? What does it mean to work together in chaotic times? When do you find joy together in these chaotic times?

Learn Together

Go to www.deepeningcommunity.com to meet other community seekers and to find more guides, exercises, and stories.

Berrett–Koehler
Publishers

Berrett-Koehler is an independent publisher dedicated to an ambitious mission: *Creating a World That Works for All*.

We believe that to truly create a better world, action is needed at all levels—individual, organizational, and societal. At the individual level, our publications help people align their lives with their values and with their aspirations for a better world. At the organizational level, our publications promote progressive leadership and management practices, socially responsible approaches to business, and humane and effective organizations. At the societal level, our publications advance social and economic justice, shared prosperity, sustainability, and new solutions to national and global issues.

A major theme of our publications is "Opening Up New Space." Berrett-Koehler titles challenge conventional thinking, introduce new ideas, and foster positive change. Their common quest is changing the underlying beliefs, mindsets, institutions, and structures that keep generating the same cycles of problems, no matter who our leaders are or what improvement programs we adopt.

We strive to practice what we preach—to operate our publishing company in line with the ideas in our books. At the core of our approach is stewardship, which we define as a deep sense of responsibility to administer the company for the benefit of all of our "stakeholder" groups: authors, customers, employees, investors, service providers, and the communities and environment around us.

We are grateful to the thousands of readers, authors, and other friends of the company who consider themselves to be part of the "BK Community." We hope that you, too, will join us in our mission.

A BK Life Book

This book is part of our BK Life series. BK Life books change people's lives. They help individuals improve their lives in ways that are beneficial for the families, organizations, communities, nations, and world in which they live and work. To find out more, visit **www.bk-life.com**.

Berrett–Koehler
Publishers

A community dedicated to creating
a world that works for all

Dear Reader,

Thank you for picking up this book and joining our worldwide community of Berrett-Koehler readers. We share ideas that bring positive change into people's lives, organizations, and society.

To welcome you, we'd like to offer you a free e-book. You can pick from among twelve of our bestselling books by entering the promotional code **BKP92E** here: http://www.bkconnection.com/welcome.

When you claim your free e-book, we'll also send you a copy of our e-newsletter, the *BK Communiqué*. Although you're free to unsubscribe, there are many benefits to sticking around. In every issue of our newsletter you'll find

- A free e-book
- Tips from famous authors
- Discounts on spotlight titles
- Hilarious insider publishing news
- A chance to win a prize for answering a riddle

Best of all, our readers tell us, "Your newsletter is the only one I actually read." So claim your gift today, and please stay in touch!

Sincerely,

Charlotte Ashlock
Steward of the BK Website

Questions? Comments? Contact me at bkcommunity@bkpub.com.

MIX
From responsible sources
FSC® C113845

Certified

Corporation
bcorporation.net